The Shift

The Shift

Choose Life, Self-knowledge Follows

Hanitra N. Ralaiarisedy

RESOURCE *Publications* • Eugene, Oregon

Resource Publications
An Imprint of Wipf and Stock Publishers
199 W. 8th Ave., Suite 3
Eugene, OR 97401

www.wipfandstock.com

PAPERBACK ISBN: 978-1-62564-515-9
HARDCOVER ISBN: 978-1-4982-8779-1
EBOOK ISBN: 978-1-7252-4919-6

Manufactured in the U.S.A.   JANUARY 6, 2020

To my son Michael

Live for a moment eternal life in the midst of time.

—EVELYN UNDERHILL

Contents

CONTENTS

CONTENTS

List of Images

Introduction

THE CHURCH IS MY "poor." I am a Christian and I wrote this book as a humble contribution to the church renewal in a world that increasingly cries for justice and equity.

In spring 2013, although I am not a Catholic, I felt compelled to respond to Pope Francis's call to serve when he mentioned the importance of personal conversion over structural or political changes for the rebuilding of the universal church. The idea of writing this book slowly matured and my desire to contribute to the church renewal stood the test of time with the affirmation of my ecumenical stance, claiming for the mutual inclusiveness of the Protestant, Catholic, and Orthodox traditions.

Intertwining the use of my personal transformation with the Scripture and theological reflections, I unveil the challenges and opportunities of Christian discipleship as well as the disruptive effect of the revelation of Christian truth in the global world. I develop my narrative in seven steps, each of them in a separate chapter.

Waken-up—Chapter 1 reveals the complexity of the existential search for "who am I" and ends with my surprising finding of being a "beloved child of God"—which I believe is true for each of us—as well as my determination to respond to that love.

Integrate—Chapter 2 narrates my attempt to live "a normal life"—that is, quenching for wholeness as a "conscious of being loved by God" in the global world—while emphasizing the personal and social challenges that it entails as well as the role that interreligious awareness plays during the whole process.

Beloved—In chapter 3, I rely on my experience to develop the concept of belovedness with the hope that the phenomenon of God's unconditional love will be more understandable/accessible to many.

Called—Chapter 4 depicts the pivotal moment during which I understood that I am called to ground my faith in Christianity. This understanding prompted my formal study of theology.

Disrupt—In chapter 5, I propose a model of the Kingdom of God on Earth (KoGoE) while shedding light on a neglected Christian truth that draws its foundation on the "living cross," (i.e., "Christ is fully with us") with its disruptive effect. The model serves as a proposal to the following question: What role would Christianity play in the building of a better world and what would that look like?

Challenged—In chapter 6, I expose my understanding of some of the barriers to the individual appropriation of God's relationship with the faithful from the Christian perspective. Chief among these barriers is the brokenness of the church.

Grateful—Chapter 7 is a tribute to those who surrounded me with their love, friendship, and/or support of many natures throughout my whole journey.

This book is both unfinished and imperfect for I started a journey that never ends. I am solely responsible for its content. I hope you will see some beauty in its imperfection.

1

The Search for "Who Am I" as a Succession of Wake-Up Calls

PUZZLED BETWEEN MADAGASCAR, FRANCE, AND THE UNITED STATES

2001–2003. I FACED THE question of my identity when, living in Paris and working as an information systems consultant with a multinational consulting firm, I obtained a US work visa and moved to San Francisco, California, in 2001. My first wake-up call occurred when Americans asked me the simple question, "Where are you from?" and I could not respond. My problem was what to base it on: citizenship, ethnicity, country of origin, last country I have moved from, skin color, cultural language, etc. My lack of practice in English increased my difficulty with the question. Indeed, I was born and raised in Madagascar but this happened over thirty-five years ago. Since then, I became a dual French-Malagasy citizen, spent more time in Europe than in my native country, and came directly from France to the United States. Even though I had become more acquainted with the French culture and identity, after hesitating for a while, I chose to make things simple and responded, "I am from Madagascar," which anyway, was also true.

My situation became challenging when some of the Americans followed up with additional questions such as, "Oh, where in the world is Madagascar? What does it look like? What origins are Malagasy people from?" Tired with my inability to respond to these pertinent questions, and eager to hasten my integration in the United States, I decided to reeducate myself about Madagascar. As a result, I developed a forty-page slide show that illustrated everything that I could learn about my native country, and which I presented to different audiences as often as I could.

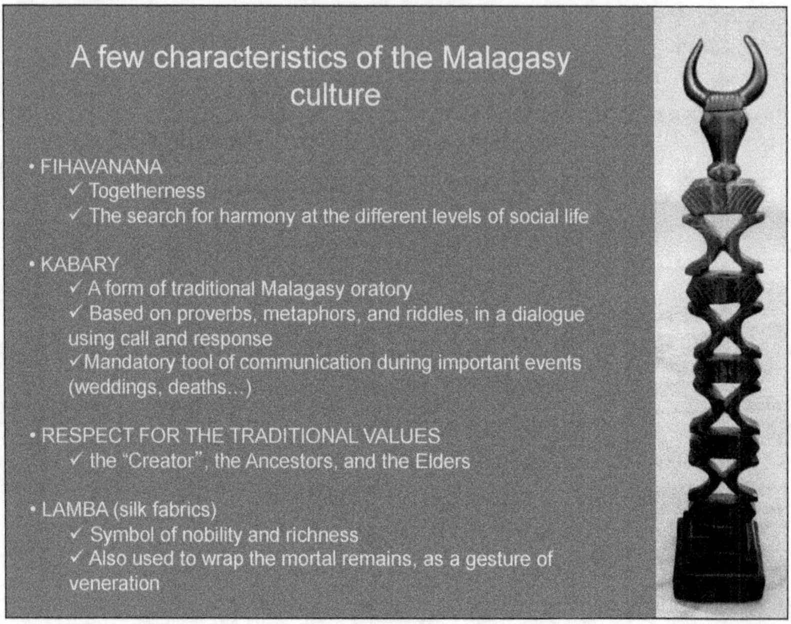

A few characteristics of the Malagasy culture

- FIHAVANANA
  - ✓ Togetherness
  - ✓ The search for harmony at the different levels of social life

- KABARY
  - ✓ A form of traditional Malagasy oratory
  - ✓ Based on proverbs, metaphors, and riddles, in a dialogue using call and response
  - ✓ Mandatory tool of communication during important events (weddings, deaths...)

- RESPECT FOR THE TRADITIONAL VALUES
  - ✓ the "Creator", the Ancestors, and the Elders

- LAMBA (silk fabrics)
  - ✓ Symbol of nobility and richness
  - ✓ Also used to wrap the mortal remains, as a gesture of veneration

Figure 01. A slide presentation on Madagascar (2003)

In addition to improving my English skills and widening my circle of American friends, this experience had the positive outcome of reconnecting me with my late ninety-year-old grandmother whom I had lost touch with.

UNITED WITH THE BEAUTY OF ISLAM
WITHOUT KNOWING

2001–2002. I met with Parisette (I use this name for the purpose of anonymity,) my first American friend, during my first days at work in the United States. She was a Turkish-born American. We never talked about religion at work. Not only was it politically incorrect but we were also focused on our integration to our new work environment. Having grown up in the United States, Parisette was very knowledgeable about the American culture and she introduced me to the American way of being and doing. Then, the dot-com crisis came and we were both mass laid-off. Our challenge turned out to be an opportunity for something more. We started opening to one another in a deeper way. Our new situation unveiled hidden/new facets of our personalities. I started paying attention to Parisette's beautiful way of expressing love and kindness to people around her. I found it fascinating and I called her the "expert of love." During one of our lazy days, we went to a bookstore in San Francisco and she introduced me to Rumi, a Persian Sufi mystic of the thirteenth century. I learned that she was Muslim. It was the first time I met with a Muslim and heard about Sufism, the mystical branch of Islam. A few months later, she decided to move back to Istanbul with her husband and I went back to business. Since then, I attended lectures on Rumi each time the occasion arose. Rumi's poetry is among the most enchanting discoveries of my life journey and so is my encounter with my beautiful Muslim friend.

CAN I BE A CHRISTIAN AND LIVE LIKE A BUDDHIST?

2002–2006. The second wake-up call took the form of a religious quest. I needed to understand what it meant to be a faithful person. Raised by Lutheran parents, Anglican grandparents and attending Catholic schools, I have naturally built my ethical foundation on Christian values. However, in early 2006, I started questioning my faith when I realized that I never evoked Christ in my prayers. Rather, I directly addressed them to God. I had no "real" place for Christ in my life and doubted about being a Christian. Then, I asked myself questions such as "Am I praying as a Jewish person or a Christian?" and "What does it mean to be a Christian?" I felt an increasing urgency to find the answers and decided to set a plan for spiritual growth. I started with a short retreat at the Jesuit Retreat Center in Los Altos, California. From that retreat, I took away the following prayer: "God, help me become a loving person."

Three months later, with my Buddhist friend, I attended my first Buddhist retreat with Thich Nhat Hanh at the "Village des Pruniers" in France. Introduced to Zen practices, I learned that mundane activities offered opportunities for meditation. However, spiritually immature, I was not able to grasp the importance of peeling vegetables or driving a car with mindfulness. I found the practice of walking meditations to be more "accessible" at that time albeit I was far from understanding their actual purpose.

As my quest went on, I started thinking that I can be a "good" Christian and live like a Buddhist. If at first I felt guilty about not praying as/like a Christian, I finally realized that doubts were essential to deepen my faith, and started apprehending the difference between spirituality and religion.

ENCOUNTER WITH IGNATIUS OF LOYOLA

I had my first Jesuit retreat at "Les Fontaines,"[1] near Paris, in spring 1996. The title "Grandir dans la liberté de nos choix," translated "Growing-up in the freedom of our choice," immediately drew my attention. Indeed, I was unable to decide whether to end a disappointing relationship with a friend. During the entire retreat, everything resonated within my being: the Ignatian spirituality immediately spoke to me, the other retreatants were charming, and the place, beautiful. At the end of the weekend, my feeling of disappointment for my friend had vanished and had never come back. I was able to peacefully handle the relationship. To my surprise, the

---

1. I find it worth sharing that due to lack of funding, the same retreat center was sold two years later to Cap Gemini Ernst & Young, the consulting firm through which I moved to the United States.

spiritual exercises worked like a magic gentle wand. Then, I went back to business as usual and forgot this episode of my life. During an errand in a Parisian bookstore, the title of a book caught my attention, *Discours d'Ignace de Loyola aux Jésuites d'aujourd'hui*, by Karl Rahner. Rahner, a Jesuit theologian and priest, considered the little book as Ignatius's testament. At that time, I was unable to understand the important messages that Rahner tried to communicate to his fellow Jesuits in Ignatius's name. Ten years later, I went to business school at the Jesuit University of San Francisco. My interest in Ignatius increased over time. Later on, I wondered how to explain such connection while I was not even a practicing Catholic.

LEARNING TO LOVE MYSELF

2008. I was introduced to the writings of Parker Palmer during my graduate studies. In his book titled *Let Your Life Speak*, Parker Palmer stated,

> My life is not only about my strengths and virtues, it is also about my liabilities and my limits, my trespasses and my shadows. . . . We must embrace what we dislike or find shameful about ourselves as well as we are confident and proud of.[2]

Palmer's approach has been illuminating to me. He helped me understand that my truths and values come primarily from "reading my life," that is, through my experience. I started getting the courage to accept every part of myself that is hurt and shameful and identifying my strengths and weaknesses in a new way. I started loving myself differently . . . or authentically.

FIRST STEP TO AUTHENTIC LEADERSHIP

2008–2009. Upon learning that authentic leadership starts with the ability to lead "oneself," I was prompted to find the response

2. Palmer, *Let your Life Speak*, 6–7.

to the unanswered "who am I" in a new context. For a long time, I have confused management and leadership. Indeed, the manager's first preoccupation is to serve the time and budget associated with a given project. S/he is rewarded based upon this criterion. On the contrary, a leader's first preoccupation is to serve people, or an ideal, or something greater than him/herself. A manager becomes a leader when s/he consciously switches from "serving time and budget" to "serving people" while meeting profitability.

This understanding reminded me of my early management experience while working for an aerospace and defense company in Paris. The project I was responsible for had met its deadlines and budget. The client rewarded me with a bonus and I happily thought that I was successful. However, a few weeks later, I had inadvertently learned that my subordinates were unhappy during the whole project. I was unable to sense their feeling. Later on, I concluded that I acted as a manager, not a leader.

A new shift occurred when I read *True North*, authored by Bill George. Ann Fudge, one of his interviewees, said:

> The challenge is to understand ourselves well enough to discover where we can use our leadership gifts to serve others. We are here for something. Life is about giving and living fully.[3]

I sensed something fundamental. It reminded me of my teenage years and St-Exupery's quote: "To be a man is precisely to be responsible. It is to feel when setting one's stone that one is contributing to the building of the world."[4] I felt the urgency to understand the leader that I am. I thought of the significant events of my life and the way I handled them: my departure from Madagascar, my early motherhood in France, my moving to the United States, etc. I concluded that vision and intuition were instrumental in modeling my career path. However, beyond these "tools," there was necessarily the presence of God. This new understanding shifted my career perspective: whereas I used to be motivated by

3. George, *True North*, XXIX.
4. St-Exupery, *Wind, Sand and Stars*, 60.

external opportunities, threats, and/or social norms, I had become "internally driven." I needed to approach my career with my authentic being.

TALES OF WONDER

2009. I received Huston Smith's newly published autobiography, *Tales of Wonder: Adventures Chasing the Divine, an Autobiography*, as a graduation gift. He was born and raised in a developing country, i.e., the Republic of China, where he lived until the age of seventeen, and he felt highly enriched by this early experience. Moreover, he did not just teach or study the world religions. He actually experimented them. Huston Smith lived in Berkeley, a thirty-minute drive from the city where I used to live at that time. Burnt with the desire to meet with Huston Smith, I sent him a letter to request an appointment and prepared all the questions that I had upon the reading of his autobiography. I carefully wrote my two-page questions. Three weeks later, I met with Huston Smith at the assisted living place where he temporarily lived in Berkeley. Beyond his knowledge of the world religions, Huston Smith captivated me with his way of tackling serious topics with kindness and fine humor. Since then, I attended the monthly meetings that he held with a group of friends until he passed away. During the meetings, each of us prepared questions that came from our readings or life experiences to which Huston joyfully, brilliantly, and humbly responded. Among his many words of wisdom and sayings, the following especially caught my attention: (1) The mind is comfortable with facts and fictions; it is not made for grasping ultimates; (2) Hinduism has identified spiritual temperaments that translate into four ways of reaching out to God: Jnanis through knowledge, Bakhtis through love, karmic types through service, and rajic types through meditation; (3) Develop your ability to hear the silence in the sound of the bell; and (4) Follow the light. These words of wisdom drew my attention for they confirmed my intuitive understanding of some truths.

THE ULTIMATE TRUTH: WE ARE THE
BELOVED CHILDREN OF GOD

2009. The most life-changing wake-up call happened when I heard Henri Nouwen's sermon "Being the Beloved." I spontaneously sensed and knew what he was talking about. He spoke my truth, a long-lost/hidden truth. I started crying, feeling both happy and confused. I felt God's love in my guts, neither in my head nor my heart, but in my guts. Overwhelmed by a deep feeling of gratitude, I sobbed. I hid my tears for I could not explain to my family what had happened. Since that moment, my quest for "who am I" definitely ended. My human needs lost their importance. If this discovery marked the end of an important step of my journey, it left me with more questions than answers. The most challenging of those questions was, "How will I respond to this love?" My concept of career shifted to mission. I felt responsible for making a difference in the world. I understood that God wanted me to become a loving person as a response to his/her love, but how? This question marked the starting point of my search for wholeness whose complexity increased with a new event, i.e., my American naturalization.

GLOBAL CITIZENSHIP: A DOUBLE-EDGED SWORD

2010. Watching the twenty-first Winter Olympic games, I surprisingly saw myself cheering the American teams that played against the French. I had always supported the French teams in the past, an "easy trade-off" as the Malagasy teams had never—or rarely—reached the final competitions. Indeed, without being naturalized, I unconsciously started "feeling" as if I was an American citizen. Two months later, I got my third citizenship, the American one. In other words, I literally became a global citizen. I saw this gift as a double-edged sword: it expanded the realm of the "possible" while increasing the complexity of my quest for wholeness.

With my business and global background, the issues of the world started coming to mind with questions such as, what happened to those leaders who lost their ethical behaviors when they faced difficult situations? What is more useful for our society, to help individuals make "good" decisions, or to promote socially responsible/sustainable businesses, etc.? Aware of the complexity of such questions, the idea of pursuing a doctoral study tickled my mind. If I had only listened to my reason, it was not the right time for further studies. I had just graduated from business school and should have, from a logical perspective, done my best to find a new well-paying job and paid back my student loans. Something was deeply different this time. I had a strong sense and understanding of something "more," something that had nothing to do with job position, money, or social status. I could even support my psychologically "uncategorized" need with sound rational explanations. From the irrational perspective, I yearned about responding to the gift of God's love with my whole and authentic being. Most importantly, I envisioned my "ideal self" as the manifestation of a total alignment with God's will. A year later, I studied Boyatzis's *intentional change theory*, in which he suggested that "conscious realization of one's ideal self may appear as a surprise or an epiphany. This emergence of a new insight or awareness is a discontinuous break with prior consciousness about one's aspirations or future."[5] I felt encouraged by such a statement. Indeed, the intentional change theory seemed to concur with the way I experienced my encounter with God's love, as well as with the way it impacted my life choices. I had defined my ideal self as "the state of total alignment with God's will." The intentional change theory would see it as the "beloved child of God." In the next chapter, I will attempt to align who I am as "beloved child of God" with my daily actions, for the purpose of finding God's will, thus my vocation.

---

5. Boyatzis, *Ideal Self*, 628.

2

Integrating Who I Am with What I Do

MORE THAN MONEY

I KNOW ONLY TWO persons who left their tenured position at Harvard University to pursue their calling. Mark Albion is one of them. I discovered Mark Albion through his book *More than Money*, in which he invited MBA graduates to develop their destiny plan by asking themselves four questions: (1) Who are you? (2) What do you want? (3) What can you do? (4) Where are you going? His first question, "Who are you," increased my interest in Mark Albion. He related the response to "Who are you" with your passion whereas I found mine as the beloved child of God. Intuitively, I saw a common point between the two concepts but the time was not right for such comparison. I had to meet with Mark Albion. Enthusiastic, I sent him an email request for a meeting, thinking that he lived in the San Francisco Bay Area. It turned out that he lived in Washington, DC. Yet, a few days later, he informed me via email of his speaking engagement at the Corporation for National and Community Services in San Francisco the following month. At the event, Mark Albion surprised me when he ended his talk by praising God. We were in the midst of a meeting with participants from both the for-profit and nonprofit sectors who presented their practices for corporate social responsibility, not at a church service. I admired Mark Albion for his faith. He abandoned a "prestigious" career to follow his truth and as a layperson, he dared to pronounce the word "God" in the business world. He showed me what is possible.

COMPLETING THE SPIRITUAL EXERCISES

Ready to live as a beloved child of God, I decided to equip myself with the most helpful tools, and the Spiritual Exercises of Saint Ignatius of Loyola came first on my list. When I discovered the Spiritual Exercises thirteen years earlier, during my first retreat in France, I understood them as a decision-making tool. The Spiritual Exercises offer much more. Thibodeaux explains,

> The Spiritual Exercises is also known as Ignatian discernment. True discernment teaches us to be self-aware . . . true discernment involves every aspect of our person, from emotion to analysis, from desire to resistance, from personal will to personal prayer.[1]

I wanted the Spiritual Exercises to help me make all my life decisions and discern God's will as a beloved child of God. As a result, I decided to complete the Spiritual Exercises in its entirety. Upon the completion of the "Exercises," and with the issues of the global world in mind, I applied for a doctoral program in management.

BRIDGING THE GAP BETWEEN BUSINESS AND SPIRITUALITY

I wanted to explore ways for incorporating spiritual values into decision-making systems and help organizational leaders make spiritually responsible decisions. At that time, very few accredited universities favored the integration of spirituality and business.

1. Thibodeaux, *God's Voice Within*, 1.

Case Western Reserve University was one of them. Unsurprisingly, my first doctoral topic related to the integration of "love" in organizational systems for sustainable development, as depicted in the following figure.

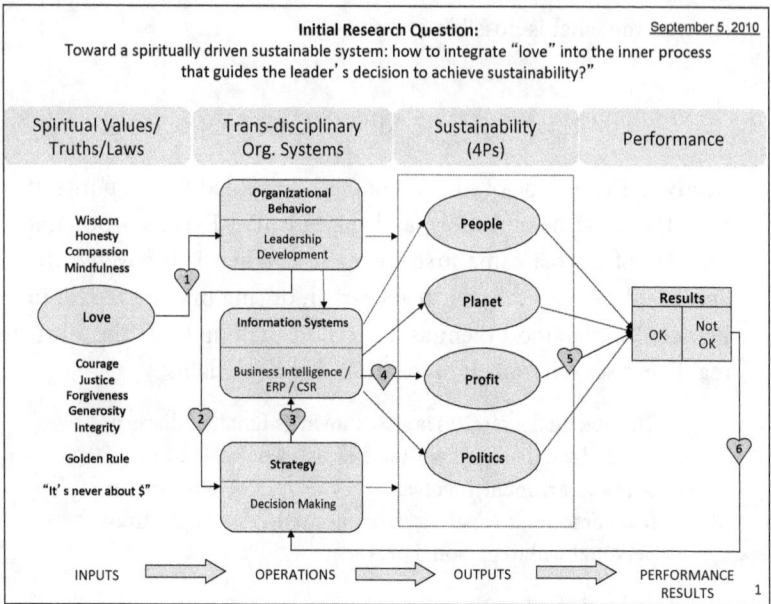

Figure 02. Presentation on Research Methods (2010)

Due to academic constraints, I had to limit my research topic to the study of the challenges and opportunities of "spiritually sensitive leaders" in the twenty-first century.

While I sometimes felt frustrated with the academic system, I enjoyed the mind-stretching element of the doctoral program at Case Western Reserve University. I further enjoyed its research-practitioner orientation for it allowed the confrontation of my lived experience with the state-of-the-art in multiple academic disciplines. Later on, I realized this confrontation is the starting point of knowledge creation. I was in my element with analytical thinking and the realm of ideas. The situation was coherent with my professional experience in the consulting industry. Everything concurred with my choice of the academic path. Yet a year later, upon the completion of the first major requirement, I quit the program despite the positive feedback that I received from my faculty advisors as well as the fellowship that I was awarded.

Unable to openly express my lack of satisfaction about the academic system, I provided my academic advisors with an explanation that represented half of the truth.

INTERRELIGIOUS DIALOGUE

The San Francisco Bay Area offered a rich exposure to a variety of interreligious events and conversations. I immersed myself in that movement through the United Religions Initiative (URI). In addition to deepening my understanding of the world religions, the URI provided me with the opportunity to experiment with different spiritual practices and introduced me to the peace-building movement. I was particularly impressed by one of the URI founding members, i.e., Sally Mahé. She did not just talk about the possibility of peace between all religions but embodies her peaceful interreligious beliefs through her professional and personal lives. As I increasingly became interested in the interreligious dialogues, I figured out that Christians who value other religious beliefs and spiritual traditions had a difficulty to define who they actually are as Christians and so did I. I think it was due to the negative connotation that Christianity has been carrying in the twenty-first century. During an interreligious gathering, our group leader, the late Margaret Jones, suggested something that I found practical and adopted at that time. She said: "When I am in interreligious settings, I call myself 'interfaith Christian' in order to avoid any misunderstanding."

A key moment occurred when I was asked to present the topic of spiritual integrity before an interreligious audience. While it usually took me several hours—nay days—to prepare for "important" presentations, I experienced something completely different that time: I prepared for the entire presentation the day before, and was ready within a couple of hours. I was filled with lightness and peaceful joy. The day of the presentation, everything went well beyond my expectations. I felt joyful and playful. I called that experience a "taste of wholeness." A few days later, I was invited to speak on the same topic before another audience. At that time, I could define "being whole" as follows: "I was the truest version of myself and I produced great results with very little efforts."

BEING GOOD OR BEING WHOLE:
WHAT'S THE DIFFERENCE?

I had to make a living but I was unclear about what to do. I had always expected to be able to live with my vocation, i.e., the "end for which I was created," but it did not happen. How to behave like a beloved child of God or how to respond to God's love? Whereas the response to such questions seems to be trivial, for it is about being in love and acting with love, its experience is far from being simple: what is love, who am I supposed to love with which love and how? These questions are challenging in the contexts of personal, social, and professional lives. Then I told myself: "If I had to die within a month, what could I do now with who I am and what I have, and nothing else?" This lead to the founding of the nonprofit "Global Passport for Orphans," whose mission was to "support organizations that help orphans and abandoned children develop their creativity and the capacity to become global citizens, fostering a culture of peace, love and justice in their communities." My aunt always wanted to take care of orphans. Within a few months after the incorporation of the nonprofit, I quickly realized that while I felt comfortable conceiving creative programs for the orphans, I disliked raising funds. Moreover, the US-based organization that was supposed to partner with us in that regard never provided any help of any nature. Upon discerning further, I concluded that I have primary launched the nonprofit as a result of "I would love to do for my family," not "I would love to do for the orphans." Then, I slowly recognized that there is a difference between "being good" and "being whole." I increasingly lost my energy. The good news: while I gave up as the cofounder of the nonprofit in the United States, my family continued the project in Madagascar completely on their own. A year later, they welcomed nineteen orphans from four months old to eleven years old to a newly built orphanage, making the learning of classical music one of the foundational activities. I interpreted this positive outcome as follows: not only did God take care of my family and the orphans, but also God prevented me from feeling guilty.

This experience made me understand the relationship between wholeness, aliveness, and creative energies. Later on, I figured out that we cannot be whole without being good. But this is another story.

THE "GOOD FEARFUL" CHRISTIAN

Leaving the orphanage behind, I took the first job that came my way, i.e., a sales position in the publishing industry. God awaited me there with another surprise.

I met with Ratatouille (I use this name for the purpose of anonymity) during my first day at work. We immediately got along with each other. A week later, I learned that he is a fervent practicing Catholic. Indeed, I saw him reading a "little book" in his car every morning. Later on, I figured out it was the Bible. We started discussing and sharing our faith as often as we could. I also realized that he was a "fearful/lawful" Christian for he emphasized the importance of sins and the law instead of God's love. He unceasingly repeated, "We must fear and respect the Lord." I found in Ratatouille someone who symbolizes the "good" Christian: he reads the Bible on a daily basis and had taken care of his sick and handicapped friend for decades. He is the one people call when they need any sort of help. Ratatouille sincerely manifests his love by deeds. However, while I admired Ratatouille's capacity to serve others, I was struck by his lack of aliveness. His health even suffered from a fearful and dutiful life. I started thinking of ways to share my understanding of Christian faith with him. I wanted to tell him that Christian faith is not just about being fearful of the law and if he continued doing so, Christ would have died for nothing. After a few weeks, I failed with all my attempts to make him understand this view. Frustrated, I decided to give up. This encounter introduced me to "fearful good Christianity."

FREEDOM IS NOT THE ABILITY TO DO WHAT I WANT, WHEN I WANT, AND WHERE I WANT

My understanding of freedom evolved over time. During my search for "who am I," I defined freedom as "the ability to do what I want, when I want, and where I want." Relatively speaking, I had reached this goal from personal and professional perspectives. Indeed, I had been living and working across industries and continents, holding various business positions. I took time for personal growth as desired. With my consulting work, I could easily take time off for vacations, discover new countries, and visit my family and friends both in Madagascar and France as often as I wanted. My son was grown up and I had few family obligations. In short, I was free from "doing" what I want, when I want, and where I want.

I developed a new understanding of freedom, which became the ability to make a living by doing something that I was passionate with. Hence, I tackled new types of consulting projects. At that time, the famous ones in the United States related to the Enron scandal, which led to the creation of Sarbanes-Oxley, a newly adopted legislation that public companies were—and still are—required to implement worldwide. I enjoyed helping my clients to comply with the new legislation, building solutions from scratch. Later on, I joined a startup company that automated the complex requirements of Sarbanes-Oxley legislation.

Then, with my practice of the Spiritual Exercises and Zen meditation, freedom became a state of indifference or nonattachment to earthly matters. Later on, freedom had become the willingness to abandon myself into God's hands. I attained the greatest freedom when I allowed God to become the "pilot," and when I can sit with boundless confidence next to him regardless of the direction. It took me several years to realize and live the form of freedom that only God can bring to our knowledge through his/

her gift of grace, i.e., Christian freedom. Indeed, one of the characteristics of Christian freedom is that it has the power to sustain all the above experience of freedom, i.e., nonattachment to earthly matters and abandonment into God's hands.

LEARNING TO BE COMPASSIONATE LIKE CHRIST

Ignatian spirituality opened a new dimension to my relationship with Christ. I started including daily Bible reading and meditative prayers into my spiritual practices, engaging in conversation with Christ, imagining and feeling the way he must have felt. I find it helpful to relate to Jesus when I remind myself of becoming a compassionate person. As I continuously learned about Christ through the reading of Scripture, he became a dear friend. A question that I asked myself and found helpful was, "What would Christ do in this situation?" Using Christ as a model, I learned to see and respond to the suffering of others to the best of my ability. As I advanced on my journey, I realized that compassion was important but it might not be the primary purpose of Christ's coming on earth. There was something else, yet something that does not diminish the value of compassion. Indeed, one can be compassionate without imitating Christ.

THIRST FOR MEANING SUSTAINS
INNER PEACE AND RESILIENCE

When the "*How* do I respond to God's love" becomes the primary preoccupation, the quest for completeness is coupled with a burning desire to find rational explanations to the "curious" facts of life (or the "*Why*"): Why do I work on this job? Why am I in the United States? Why do I feel loved by God and others do not? Why do I have three citizenships? Why can I be at my best on certain activities with little effort and my worst on others? And most importantly, why am I on earth?

After a while, unable to find satisfying answers to the "*Why*" questions, I decided to switch to "*What*": What is my best way to respond to God's love? As a beloved child of God, what can I do with my current situation? Thus, I started making an inventory of what I had and gave "what I have" (i.e., time, skills, and money) until I understood it was about giving myself or giving the "*Who*" I am. Later on, I realized my search for meaning sustains peace. Indeed, as soon as I found the meaning of a specific experience, no matter how challenging it is, I had a sense of inner peace.

The search for meaning helped me analyze my experience and find rational explanations to unanswered questions after the fact. I started recognizing patterns of experience that progressively built my self-confidence and resilience. Furthermore, I see a possible relationship between the search for meaning and my understanding of the phenomenon of grace in the sense that I am co-responsible with God. Indeed, God seems to need both my "passive and active" participation in order to make certain things happen.

"SPIRITUAL DIRECTION" MAKES A DIFFERENCE

I had the privilege to learn from several spiritual guides and companions with multiple and diverse skills. Each of them played specific roles at different steps of my spiritual journey. The variety of their skills was instrumental in enriching the multiple contexts in which I grew spiritually. Most importantly, they helped in the confirmation of my understanding of each step of my spiritual path until it had become an affair between God and me alone.

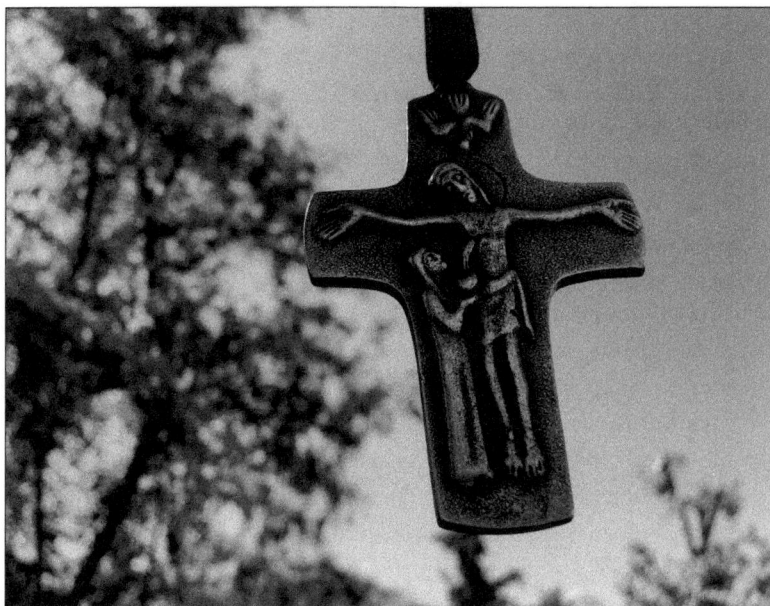

Figure 03. A gift from Mary Manning, spiritual director

One thing worth sharing that my spiritual directors had in common is their generosity. They generously offered their guidance and time for free. Moreover, none of them has ever said "no" when I was in need of a listening heart and of reaching out for a conversation or a meeting. What mattered to my spiritual guides was the nurturing of our respective personal experience and relationship with God.

This experience demonstrates that even though things are sometimes broken at the institutional level, wonderful things happen at the individual level. With all these gifts, I realized God manifests his/her love through people around me in multiple ways. The gift of spiritual direction is definitely one of them.

A CALL FOR JUSTICE

Five years after my encounter with God, I have accumulated over $200K in student loans. Upon discerning my situation, I decided to apply for bankruptcy in summer 2014. The complex relationship between money and spirituality is not something new. Yet did I need to live this asocial, negative, nay shameful, experience of bankruptcy? Does it hide a higher meaning or is it merely a self-destructive behavior that pertains to a psychological-related issue? As I reflected on my relationship with money, some truths progressively emerged. I have been always "financially unwise." To say it in another way, financial management is one of my Achilles heels. I may even say my "sins." For example, whether I earn $100k annual salary or $0k, I always ended up with $0 at the end of the year. In the meantime, I had been always lucky with money during my professional life. I easily found well-paying jobs and regularly increased my salary. Yet, I had never really paid attention to God's gift of money. I took it for granted. Things started being out of my control when I engaged on the spiritual path. I have never been able to make a living with spiritual-related activities. Each time I expected to make a living with my vocation, something beyond my control prevented it from happening. Moreover, if spiritual maturity meant the ability to feel comfortable in a business setting while pursuing a religious quest, I have not attained that state of being. Indeed, I increasingly felt both inadequate and frustrated each time I had to go back to the business world. As I reflected on my situation, a light slowly emerged. God would have not asked me to undertake this risky journey if I was not of an adventurous nature. God would have never asked me to learn to feel abundant with no money if I was not able to make money. This situation reminded me of a biblical message: "No temptation has overtaken you except what is common to mankind. And God is faithful; he will not let you be tempted beyond what you can bear. But when you are tempted, he will also provide a way out so that you can endure it" (1 Cor 10:13).

Hence, God's plan started making sense in a perfectly rational way. I started understanding that I had to learn to be both vulnerable and courageous. I had to unveil a systemic injustice in relation to my personal situation, namely, a case of injustice that pertains to the bankruptcy legislation in the United States. Here is the issue:

If someone borrowed $1M for a business purpose and applied for bankruptcy, the US legislation would totally forgive the business loan. On the contrary, a student loan would not benefit from that forgiveness. In other words, the student would still have to pay the loan in its entirety. This case has been recently made public and my situation is far from being an isolated one. I wonder how many of the other students are in search for their life purpose. I am calling for justice and equity.

3

Belovedness

A "BELOVED SELF" IS WORTH EXAMINING

2013 ONWARD. FOUR YEARS after my encounter with God's love, I needed to formalize and share my experience of being loved by God. I drew on biblical inspiration to develop the concept of "belovedness," as depicted in the figure below.

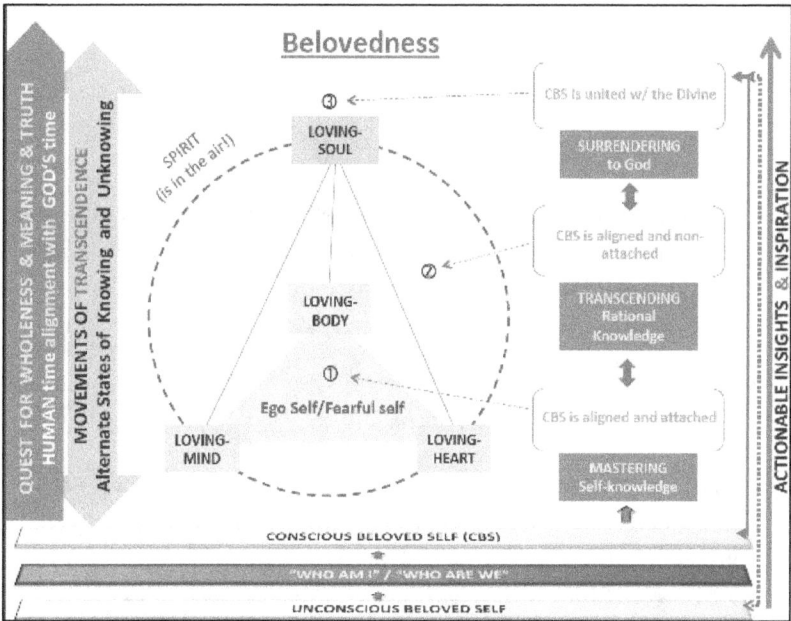

Figure 04. A working conceptual model of Belovedness

An encounter with God's love triggers a quest for completeness/ wholeness. In that context, I define a quest for completeness as "a human process of transformation that starts with a personal encounter with God's love and aims at intentionally returning that love by finding, then living one's truth(s) with love and without compromise." My response to God's love leads me to the teaching of the Bible as a first step.

HUMAN LOVE

Belovedness relies on the biblical definition of love in 1 Cor 13:4–7, as it is translated in the New International Version as follows:

> *Love is patient, love is kind. It does not envy, it does not boast, it is not proud. It does not dishonor others, it is not self-seeking, it is not easily angered, it keeps no record of wrongs. Love does not delight in evil but rejoices with the*

truth. It always protects, always trusts, always hopes, always perseveres.

Beloved Self

I describe the experience of beloved self through the lens of relationship, i.e., relationship with myself, with God, with others, (and with nature). Beloved self is composed of a loving-soul, a loving-heart, a loving-mind, a loving-body . . . and an (hidden) ego self.

Loving-Mind

I use my loving-mind when I rely on my intellect to express love. As such, loving-mind is able to rationally explain the motive of my loving intentions and actions. I can say, "I love myself and I love you and/or I love God *because* . . ." Per my adoption of the biblical definition, loving-mind pertains to the rational aspect of love, i.e., *"love does not envy, it does not boast, it is not proud. It does not dishonor others, it is not self-seeking, it is not easily angered, it keeps no record of wrongs."*

Loving-Heart

I use my loving-heart when I am able to feel and act upon God's love and my love for God. Here, feeling necessarily precedes action. Per my adoption of the biblical definition, loving-heart is *"patient and kind. It always protects, always hopes, always trusts, always perseveres."* Loving-heart is the source of compassion and forgiveness.

Loving-Body

I use my loving-body when I rely on my five senses (i.e., smelling, touching, hearing, seeing, tasting) to express love. Loving-body is the most visible part of my beloved self. Thus, it manifests the most tangible—or socially understood—expression of love.

When loving-heart and loving-mind are not able to "listen," loving-body finds ways to "speak" or react.

Loving-Soul

Loving-soul is the path (i.e., "narrow gate"?) to God's mystery. Loving-soul is the most hidden part of my beloved self for it does not have any physical support—or organ—such as the heart, body and/or brain. That makes the loving-soul the most delicate part of my beloved self to grasp. It requires a total abandonment to God. With loving-soul, I am called to receive rather than to achieve. Loving-soul is totally under God's control.

Ego Self or Fearful Self

Ego is a fearful reaction of loving-mind. Fear is the opposite of love. Consequently, fear negates the biblical definition of love as follows:

> Fear is not patient, fear is not kind. It envies, it boasts, it is proud. It dishonors others, it is self-seeking, it is easily angered, it keeps record of wrongs. Fear delights in evil and does not rejoice with the truth. It does not protect, does not trust, does not hope, does not persevere.

I manifest my fear/ego through the loving-mind (thought), loving-heart (feeling), and/or loving-body (behavior).

Spirit

Drawing from the biblical teaching, Spirit with "S" is the Holy Spirit whereas spirit with "s" relates to human knowledge or intelligence. Therefore, there is one Spirit for all of us and as many spirits as there are human beings. In the concept of belovedness, Spirit relates to the Holy Spirit. Spirit is pervasive. It is available to everyone and can be received through loving-mind, loving-heart, loving-body and/or loving-soul.

Attachment

Attachment is a thought, feeling or sensation that leads to the disturbance of loving-mind, loving-body and/or loving-heart. It derives from ego self/fearful self. Attachment leads to loss of inner peace.

Attachment of Loving-Heart

Attachment of the loving-heart has a specific nature. Loving-heart gives me a taste of agape (i.e., unconditional love.) However, depending on the nature of the interpersonal relationship, an "attached" loving-heart can disturb my inner peace. In that case, the Spirit transforms loving-heart into an *intelligent heart*, i.e., a heart that both loves and knows the "truth" about the situation at hand.

Alignment

Alignment means loving-mind, loving-heart and loving-body all together say "yes" to what I intend to do. Alignment awakens my creative energies (i.e., actionable insights and inspiration), which I am happy to share/communicate with people around me. Moreover, alignment does not necessarily prevent loving-heart, loving-mind and loving-body from being attached to something/ someone. Hence, alignment and attachment follow different human processes. Once tasted, reflected and experimented, alignment becomes a way of being, not just a habit of mind.

Alignment with God's Time

In addition to the state of harmony between loving-mind, loving-heart and loving-body, as well as the awakening of creative energies, I am aligned with God's time when I have no expectation about the future and simply attend to the daily aspects of my life in a peaceful and loving way. I feel highly comfortable with the unknown. Alignment with God's time is confirmed by mysterious and synchronistic events (involving people, place and activity) that make the moment just "perfect."

Transcendence

Transcendence applies to loving-mind which governs loving-body and loving-heart. The act of transcendence implies the existence of "lots of things"—as opposed to "nothing"—to transcend. In the concept of belovedness, transcendence applies to rational knowledge.

With the participation of loving-mind, I transcend rational knowledge, i.e., I consciously stop thinking and analyzing, two habits that pertain to my natural way of being. Rather, through prayers and the reading of Scripture, I submit the myriad of creative insights that occupy my loving-mind to God. Indeed, creative insights can be a form of spiritual pride. In this context, transcendence is a form of humility before God. It removes the temptation of thinking that I am as knowledgeable as God. In transcendence, I direct my intention to the glory of God.

Surrender

Surrender is the total abandonment of my loving-mind, loving-heart and loving-body to God's will. I do nothing but engage in the practice of loving prayers towards/for God. Loving-soul is in charge.

BELOVEDNESS AS A LIVED EXPERIENCE: FIVE LEVELS OF BELOVEDNESS

Belovedness encompasses the cultivation of self-knowledge, i.e., the knowledge of each component of the beloved self (i.e., loving-mind, loving-heart, loving-body, and ego self) as well as the movements of the Spirit that guide each of them, separately and/or all together.

I identify five levels of belovedness, or five patterns of behavior of the beloved self that engages in relationship as follows: Unconscious beloved self, conscious beloved self (CBS), CBS is aligned but attached, CBS is aligned and non-attached, and CBS is united with the divine.

Unconscious Beloved Self

When I identify myself as a global citizen, or woman, or information systems consultant, or mother, or Protestant, or Christian, or Buddhist or interfaith Christian, or all of them, I am an "unconscious beloved self," that is, I do not understand, feel and/or sense God's love albeit I am always united with God.

Conscious Beloved Self (CBS)

I am a "conscious beloved self" when my life priority becomes the search for the best way to respond to God's love. Although I am conscious of being loved by God, I am unable to feel, sense and understand the difference between the movements of my loving-heart, loving-mind and loving-body. Further, I am not conscious of my ego-driven intentions and actions. In other words, I lack self-knowledge. As a result, I follow societal rules by being "good." I mostly operate from "I have to" and/or "I should do"; I lack inner peace for I intuitively know something is scattered within me. There is something more, which I am not able to understand, feel, sense, or express; I am uncomfortable with the "unknown," i.e., the things that I cannot control with my loving-mind.

CBS Is Aligned but Attached

I start knowing the difference between "being good" and "being complete." I feel the urgency to love others without sacrificing my sense of completeness. While my loving-heart, loving-mind and loving-body are aligned (i.e., I am full of creative insights and peak experiences), they still feel "attached" from time to time to earthly matters (i.e., my old way of life, expectations from others, vulnerability to judgments, etc.). My experiential understanding of my truths is confirmed through reading of Scripture, the life of the saints and/or the teaching of spiritual masters from different spiritual traditions. I know myself, i.e., I am aware of the difference between the reaction of my ego self as opposed to the reaction of my beloved self. Yet, I do not always act upon this self-knowledge. I develop the ability to be comfortable with the unknown. I privilege the desire of my loving-heart over my loving-mind when acting as a response to God's love. I am able to listen to my loving-body when it attempts to tell me some truth.

CBS Is Aligned and Non-attached

I cultivate the ability to love everything equally while solely focusing on activities and relationships that please my loving-heart regardless of the situation. Hence, I reach alignment by letting my loving-heart lead. Aligned, I am conscious of co-creating with God and accept that I cannot always explain certain phenomenon. I am comfortable with the unknown. I am aware of the difference between the reaction of my ego self as opposed to the reaction of my beloved self and I learn to act upon this awareness. I tend to ignore humanly or socially created rules as a sign of nonattachment to earthly matters and affirm my choice of living my truth(s) as a response to God's love. Hence, I transcend rational knowledge as abovementioned. This is the "step" of trials. It leads to ascetic behaviors, which make sense only to those who have reached this level of belovedness. As a result, I "have gotten rid of" everything—and everyone—that does no longer resonate with my truth(s) which, at first, is a painful experience until it becomes a liberating one. Due to the challenges that arise from a relational perspective, intelligence of the heart is of utmost importance with this level of belovedness. I multiply opportunities to see the beauty in all God's creation with gratitude.

CBS Is United with the Divine

Loving-soul is in charge through God's grace. Conscious union with the divine is cultivated through silence and the practice of loving prayers for God. I am comfortable with the unknown. I am fully in tune with my true nature as God's creative partner, albeit I am not fully aware of Christ's indwelling presence in me. An example of manifestation of that union is the act of forgiving one's "enemy," a capacity that lies beyond my loving-heart and loving-mind. Loving-soul is in charge.

Belovedness: a Singular experience?

As I shared the belovedness model around me, I increasingly realized that the immediate encounter with God's love is not a common experience. Hence, the thirst to respond to such love is not common either. I spoke with one of my friends who suggested that "we are love" (i.e., we identify ourselves as "love,") whether we are loved or not by God. I replied, "I don't know how to be 'love' if I was not first 'loved by God.'"

In the following chapter, I will narrate the pivotal moment during which I understood that I am called to ground my faith in Christianity.

4

Called to Glorify God through Christianity

FRENCH BIBLE STUDIES IN SILICON VALLEY

I BECAME AWARE OF Christ's gift of justification, for the first time, while preparing for a Bible study meeting with a group of friends. Whereas I started understanding the meaning of the gift and got excited, most of my friends didn't share my feeling about the Bible verses that we studied that evening—which I summarize as follows: we are justified by faith, not by the work of the law (Galatians 3). Instead, the message created a tension among our group. One of our friends could not accept the fact that one can be "saved" even though one does not respect the law. At that time, none of us was aware of the subtle distinction between salvation and justification, a topic that I explored a few years later during my theological studies.

ENCOUNTER WITH CHRIST DURING
A ZEN SESSHIN

In the midst of a Zen retreat led by Fr. Gregory Mayers at Mercy Center in Burlingame, California, I suddenly felt overwhelmed by a deep and strong feeling of gratitude for Christ and my ancestors who introduced me to the Christian faith . . . I sobbed. The experience reminded me of my encounter with God's love four years earlier. After a few years of Zen meditative practices, I had become used to eliminating my thoughts and emotions during those meditative moments. Hence, my feeling of gratitude for Christ and my ancestors came as a real surprise. Upon discerning that experience with the support of Fr. Gregory Mayers, I progressively understood that I was called to deepen my relationship with God through Christianity, not through interreligious endeavors. I knew both fields are not mutually exclusive. Instead, this experience had the effect of grounding my response to God's love in Christ.

Since then, I decided to stop Zen meditative practices, not because they were "useless" or "inappropriate." I had so much benefited from the Zen tradition. Instead, I wanted to deepen my understanding of Christ's calling and the truth about Christianity. What does Christ want from me? Why? Hence, I focused my spiritual endeavors on Christianity and started thoroughly experimenting with the Christian tools at my disposal: Ignatius's *Suscipe* prayer, the reading of Scripture which I complete with a daily mini–Bible study[1]—edited by a group of French ecumenical pastors and scholars—that is, an annual gift from my parents. These practices multiplied my "encounters" with the biblical characters and awakened my interest in the topic of revelation. Meanwhile, I started feeling overwhelmed by my understanding of the biblical messages as well as the one of my unveiling role. I was not sure about what to do with all my thoughts and evolving knowledge. I could not and should not keep them for myself. I started thinking of writing a book. It was during that time of abundant questioning that Karl Rahner, the Jesuit theologian and priest, came to my life once again, for the second time. As a quick reminder, I discovered

---

1. Pigeaud and Vergniol, *Parole pour Tous.*

the work of Karl Rahner for the first time in a Parisian bookstore upon the completion of my first Jesuit retreat, twelve years ago.

FROM BIBLICAL REVELATION
TO THEOLOGICAL STUDIES

I entered one of the many libraries at Mercy Center and saw an entire wall filled with some of Rahner's *Theological Investigations* in twenty-three volumes. One of the books, *Hearers of the Word*, immediately caught my attention for it alluded to the topic of revelation. The reading of Rahner's *Hearers of the Word*, which I complemented with *Unfolding Revelation: The Nature of Doctrinal Development* (Walgrave, 1972), and *Revelation and Theology* (Schillebeeckx, 1967), confirmed my experiential understanding of the phenomenon as well as the responsibility that awaited me. I understood that theological studies were necessarily to be my next step.

I finalized my investigation with the reading of Ignatius's autobiography. The latter reinforced my understanding of my calling. As a result, I decided to apply for theological studies at the Jesuit School of Theology in Berkeley, California. I intended to get from the "experts" the confirmation of my experience as a recipient of revelation while deepening my knowledge of the Scripture and Ignatian spirituality.

REFLECTIVE PRACTICE

We had to write our first reflection while attending a course on Ignatian Spirituality. Here is an excerpt:

> It has been a month since I started my theological studies at the JST, a month full of discoveries, frustrations and confirmations. The four courses that I enrolled in for the semester offer diverse perspectives that mold the diversity of my experience into a coherent whole, albeit not without difficulty.

Although I do not like the "quizzes" form of assignment, I enjoy discovering the theories that shaped the Christian ethics over the past century. Among the ethicists whom I recently discovered, Bonhoeffer stands as one of my favorites. I see his work as fostering bridges between Christians on important issues such as the theology of grace. For example, I see similar thoughts between his "penultimate reality" and Ignatius's love of the extremes for the *Magis*. I enjoy such discovery for it marks my encounter with the truth, the one that stands the test of time, the one that always comes into fruition at the right time, at God's time.

I also find it interesting to look at the Pauline corpus through the lenses of both contemporary and ancient theologians. But I mostly enjoy understanding Paul's experience through my own life. . . .

I enjoy discovering the two models that bind faith and culture in "Ignatian Vision and Cultures," namely, the "religious character of culture" and the "cultural character of religion." Such a distinction deeply resonates with my personal experience. Indeed, to what extent does my global experience influence my spiritual quest? Is there any known relationship here?

I like to affirm that the purpose of Ignatian Spirituality is to foster a personal encounter with God. The Spiritual Exercises have been, and still are, for many people, considered as a decision-making tool, which is half true. However, [. . .] Ignatius would say: "Do not confound the means with the end." Indeed, decision-making is the means whereas personal conversion through an encounter with God is the end. On the same note, I am curious about the three stages of Ignatian Spirituality, i.e., purgative, illuminative and apostolic (not unitive). Why should the apostolic character of Ignatian Spirituality be exclusive of the Union with the Divine? I sense that authentic apostolic endeavors are meant to be unitive with the divine as well. . . .

I enjoy reading this passage from the Lenten digital prayer:[2] "We all need a place inside ourselves where there is no noise, where the voice of the Spirit of God can speak

2. Fassett et al., "Moved to Greater Love," 1.

to us, softly and gently, and direct our discernment. In a very true sense we need the ability to become ourselves—silence, emptiness, an open space that the Word of God can fill, and the Spirit of God can set on fire for the good of others and of the Church. More than ever, every Jesuit should be able to live like a monk in the middle of the noise of the city—as an Orthodox friend of ours once said. That means that our hearts are our monasteries and at the bottom of every activity, every reflection, every decision, there is silence, the kind of silence that one shares only with God."

On Truth . . . Which truth to tell and which one to keep at this specific time of my journey? Does the Scripture offer guidance in that situation?

On Gratitude . . . I am filled with gratitude each time I think of my great grandparents and grandparents who embodied the values of love, hope and charity during their lifetime. I am grateful for the way God manifests his love through the people I encounter every day. I am learning to see God in the simple aspects of my life.

Five years have passed since my first reflection in theological school. Upon the completion of a consulting assignment, I felt ready to go back to the writing of this book. Greece came my way. At the end of February 2019, I landed on the Island of Kos, the birthplace of Hippocrates.

INTRODUCTION TO ORTHODOX THEOLOGY

As I followed the itinerary of the beautiful monasteries of Kos Island, something struck me: Orthodoxy has integrated the relationship between the author of the Fourth Gospel—that is, "Saint John the Evangelist"—and the author of the biblical Apocalypse, whom they call "Saint John the Theologian." Orthodoxy demonstrates such relationship through the different names under which they baptize their monasteries. Upon visiting the different monasteries, I understood that the Orthodox tradition sees Saint John the Evangelist and Saint John the Theologian as the same "historical person" and their "roles" evolved over time. Indeed, the "young"

evangelist—to whom the truths of the gospel had been revealed—
became the "old" theologian who announced the Apocalypse.

Figure 05. Agios Theologos, Kos Island, Greece

I still wanted to ensure that my interpretation of the "symbol" behind the monasteries was correct and decided to meet with the Bishop of Kos Island. I met with one of his collaborators who confirmed that the two "Saint Johns" were indeed the same historical person. He further claimed that Orthodoxy is of ecumenical nature *de facto*, which pleased me. We further continued the conversation and I inquired about the transformative process through which Saint John the Evangelist became Saint John the Theologian from the Orthodox perspective. That was obviously an unexpected question. After an animated conversation, he asked for my email address for the purpose of sending me some materials. Two days later, I received an email that contained hundreds of pages of academic literature on Orthodox theology. My heart was filled with gratitude. I gave a call to the gracious collaborator of the Bishop of Kos and thanked him for his precious gift: he offered me an unexpected introduction to Orthodox theology! After my five-year immersion in Catholic and Protestant scholarship, I realized Orthodoxy was an important missing piece from my theological and ecumenical background.

DISCOVERING AN ECUMENICAL ISSUE
THROUGH THE CULTURAL LENS

I find it important to emphasize that the two representations of Saint John (i.e., "Evangelist" and "Theologian") seem to have been integrated into the Greek mundane culture. Here is why. I visited the church of "Saint-Jean de Montmartre" in Paris, France, the previous year, in January 2018. It is a small church located at the bottom of the notorious "Basilique du Sacré-Coeur." As such, one can easily miss the less famous "Saint-Jean de Montmartre." Inside the latter, an exhibit took place and one of the display panels caught my attention.

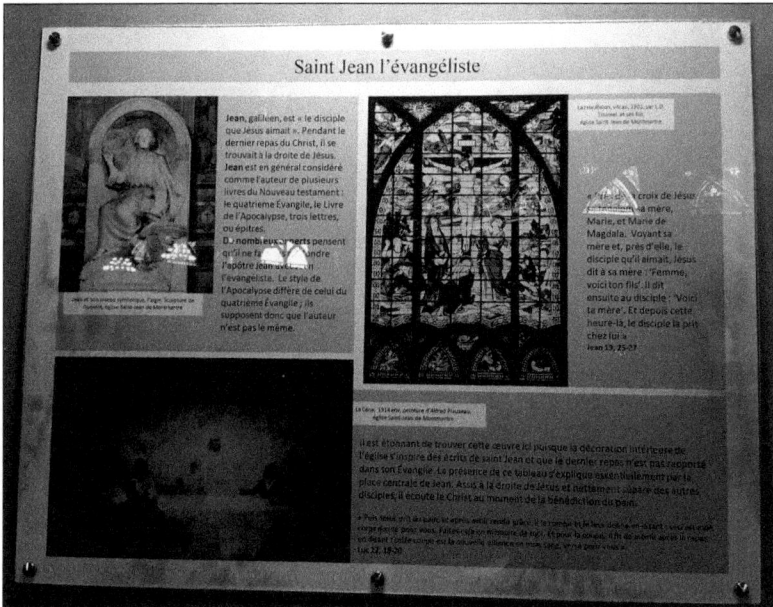

Figure 06. A display panel at l' Eglise Saint-Jean de Montmartre, Paris

The above display explains that a debate persists among the "experts" as to whether John the Evangelist and the author of the Apocalypse were the same person. In other words, there is a difference of understanding between the Orthodox and Western biblical schools of thought in that regard. My visit to the Orthodox monasteries made me understand that Orthodoxy has apprehended the biblical "truth" at least from a cultural perspective. On the contrary, the topic is still under debate in the Western school of thought.

5

Disruptive Revelation of Christian Truth

Each icon is a revelation of Christ, Who is a revelation of God the Father of Whom "no man has anywhere seen." This is then in visual form the Mystery that was before the ages, and which can never be solved, but may be pierced and thus bring us into this Mystery by entering the paradox of God and Man brought together in the Incarnation of Our Lord Jesus Christ.[1]

1. Bergenske, "Community of Joseph Icon Description."

Figure 07. Icon of the Community of Joseph

WHAT IS MISSING?

ATHENS, GREECE, ON JUNE 5, 2019. As I contemplated the Orthodox icon, which I was offered eight years ago by the Community of Joseph,[2] I suddenly realized that something of importance was

---

2. Community of Joseph is an interreligious community founded by the late Professor André Delbecq in California.

missing from my whole book. Indeed, I had naturally used the existential question "Who am I?" as the starting point of my quest. This naturally and necessarily led to my quest for self-knowledge and explained my natural inclination to Ignatian spirituality. It is no secret, the Spiritual Exercises of Ignatius of Loyola is not for everyone albeit diverse and multiple efforts have been/are being conducted to make them as such. For the reader who chose to ignore my previous chapters, I will give a quick background on Ignatian spirituality here. According to Ignatius, a spiritual exercise is

> every way of examining one's conscience, of meditating, of contemplating, of praying vocally and mentally, and of performing other spiritual actions. . . . For as strolling, walking, and running are bodily exercises, so every way of preparing and disposing the soul to rid itself of all the disordered tendencies, and after it is rid, to seek and find the Divine Will as to the management of one's life to the salvation of the soul, is called a spiritual exercise.[3]

Ultimately, Ignatius invites us to desire and choose what is most conducive to the "end for which we are created" for God's glory, namely, our life vocation. For that purpose, he relies upon self-knowledge. The latter is the indispensable component of his spirituality. I looked around me and among my five closest friends whom I see as "serious" spiritual seekers, only one of them had completed the Spiritual Exercises. He was a former Jesuit who left the novitiate over fifty years ago!

Similarly, Luther, the Reformer, sees self-knowledge as the beginning of Christian life.[4] He states: "The first step in Christianity is the reaching of repentance and the knowledge of oneself. . . . Once a man has been humbled by the law and brought to the knowledge of himself, then he becomes truly repentant; for true repentance begins with fear and with the judgment of God" (*LW* 26:126–31). According to Luther, obedience to the law has a specific purpose, that is, to advance one's self-knowledge through

---

3. Fleming, *Draw Me Into Your Friendship*, 4.
4. Ralaiarisedy, "Re-opening the Gift of Justification-by-Faith," 28.

discovery of one's sinful nature. Now, of chief importance for Luther is the justification of the faithful.

> From a theological perspective, justification takes root in our subjective appropriation of the gospel message. "Luther says: 'We are justified solely by faith in Christ . . . and the Holy Spirit is solely granted by hearing the message of the Gospel with faith . . .' (LW 26:208). The time when we hear the Word with faith in Christ corresponds to the event, that 'mysterious' moment of realization of our justified status before God. It is mysterious for it makes us understand for the first time who Christ is and why he came to earth two thousands years ago. It is truly mysterious, for this historical Jesus becomes a human being who manifests his presence to us as one to whom we can relate at the present moment. Hence, the event of Justification corresponds to our 'actual' encounter with Jesus Christ in faith through the hearing of the Word by God's free gift of grace. Mannermaa identified that encounter as a real presence of Christ in faith, or faith as the indwelling presence of Christ (Mannermaa, Christ Present in Faith, Loc. 212–217). Moreover, the event of justification marks the starting point of Luther's Happy Exchange—that is, exchange between human and divine natures, an ongoing process that Luther compares to a tree.[5]

He states:

> For those people who have already begun to be Christians. . . . It is of no value for a tree to grow green and produce blossoms, unless it also bears fruit from the blossom. Therefore, many die in the blossom stage. (*LW* 25:433–34)

This metaphor implies different degrees of progress in the Christian life where the knowledge of self as sinful is the initial step.

While I recognize the importance of self-knowledge, Ignatius and Luther's viewpoints leave me unsatisfied. Something is

---

5. Ralaiarisedy, "Re-opening the Gift of Justification-by-Faith," 19–20.

incomplete, nay unfair, and raises rhetorical questions: isn't God equitable? Do all of us need to search for and/or know ourselves in order to know God's love or God's will? What about those people who do not have the desire to know themselves, or those who, for different reasons, are not just given the ability to engage in that search? Should they be refused the knowledge of God's love or do they have to make some kind of efforts to get to such knowledge? I do not think so. These reflections brought me back to the teaching of the Bible and the full meaning of Christ's coming on earth.

THE NEGLECTED TRUTH OF THE GOSPEL: "CHRIST IS FULLY WITH US"

In the Old Testament, the prophet Isaiah announced: "Behold a virgin shall be with child, and shall bring forth a son, and they shall call his name Em-man'u-el" (Isa 7:14). While this biblical verse is well known among Christian believers, we often forget one of its crucial linkages with the New Testament. Indeed, at the beginning of his testimony, Matthew added: "Emmanuel—which being interpreted is: *God with us*" (Matt 1:23). This means that through Incarnation, Christ not only represents God, but he also does it by "being with us." God offers us the *free gift of relationship* here and now through Christ. Hence, through Christ, God stays in relationship "with us" whether we want and know it—or not. In short, *Christ is fully with us!*

From the above reflection, we can deduct that the most important question here is not whether "Christ is fully divine and fully human" (i.e., Chalcedonian doctrine), a doctrine that has been the subject of theological debates and divergences for millennia. Rather, what we need to focus on in the postmodern era is the question of God's relationship with us through Christ. I like emphasizing that gift—"Christ is fully with us"—for it reflects God's equity and justice. Indeed, as previously mentioned, the gift of relationship is offered to any of us *de facto*. It is not a future event. It is at our disposal, here and now through the Trinitarian love, to which we turn.

TRINITARIAN LOVE

God's love is first made tangible through Christ's Event (i.e., incarnation, death, and resurrection). John the Evangelist claims: "For God so loved the world that He gave His one and only Son, that whoever believes in him shall not perish but have eternal life" (John 3:16). But Christ equally loves us. "As the Father hath loved me, so have I loved you; Continue ye in my love" (John 15:9). Christ's death and resurrection makes his love tangible, and by believing in him, i.e., the mystery of his death and resurrection, we are given eternal life as abovementioned. Christ further promises to send the third component of the Trinity, i.e., the Holy Spirit, or the Spirit of Truth, to those who love him. He states: "If you love me, keep my commands. And I will ask the Father, and he will give you another advocate to help you and be with you forever—the Spirit of Truth" (John 14:15–16). Christ reiterates the message in John 14:26: "But the Advocate, the Holy Spirit, whom the Father will send in my name, will teach you all things and will remind you of everything that I have said to you."

In summary, through the Trinitarian love, we inherit eternal life and/or the Spirit of Truth in proportion to our belief and/or love for Christ as follows: the believers in Christ inherit eternal life whereas the lovers of Christ inherit both eternal life and the Spirit of Truth. Most importantly, the Trinitarian love allows for Christ's unbreakable relationship with us, here and now, regardless of how well we know ourselves. Now if Christ is fully with us, what is his presence for? To that we turn.

THE DOUBLE GIFT: KINGDOM OF GOD
AND KINGDOM OF GOD ON EARTH

Not only is Christ fully with us so that by believing in him, we can inherit eternal life, but he does so for something else/more—that is, to announce the good news of the "kingdom of God." He claims: "I must preach the kingdom of God to other cities also: for therefore am I sent" (Luke 4:43). However, in the Fourth Gospel, Christ adds some prerequisites to the access to the kingdom of God. He says: "Very truly I tell you, no one can enter the kingdom of God unless they are born of water and the Spirit. . . . Except a man be born of water and of the Spirit he cannot enter into the kingdom of God. . . . That which is born of the flesh is flesh. That which is born of the Spirit is spirit" (John 3:5–6). In other words, the access to the kingdom of God is subject to certain conditions. It is reserved to those who not only are "born again" but also "born of water and of the Spirit." Regardless of what these requirements mean, its conditional nature makes us understand something about the kingdom of God: the "kingdom of God" is not suitable to the actualization of "Christ is fully with us," the latter being God's free—and unconditional—gift of relationship with us that is at our disposal, here and now, through the Trinitarian love.

Consequently, we need to create/unveil a second kingdom, namely, the Kingdom of God on Earth (KoGoE). This fulfills Matthew's prayer, "Our Father in heaven, hallowed be your name, your kingdom come, your will be done, on earth as it is in heaven" (Matt 6:9–10). Now, what is the KoGoE?

KOGOE: WHERE DIVINE (UNCREATED) ENERGIES BECOME CO-CREATIVE OPPORTUNITIES

According to the teaching of Gregory Palamas,[6]

> There is a distinction-in-unity between God's essence and His energies. The divine essence signifies God's absolute transcendence, and we humans will never participate in it, either in this life or in the age to come. The divine energies, on the other hand, permeate the entire creation and we humans, participate in them by grace (§§65, 78).

6. I discovered Gregory Palamas, a theologian of the late Byzantine era, during the 2019 Lenten season in Kos Island, Greece. Since I neither speak nor read the Greek language, I used to get some information about the Orthodox Liturgy (of the day) before attending church service. The second Sunday of Lenten season is the Feast of Gregory Palamas in the Orthodox tradition. Since then, I have become interested in the work of Gregory Palamas, and especially in his concepts of divine essence and uncreated energies.

Thus, deification (theosis) and union with God signifies union with God's energies, not His essence (§75). That which the energies effect and produce is created, but the divine energies themselves are supernatural, eternal and uncreated (§§72–73).[7]

Drawing from Palamas's teaching, I suggest that KoGoE allows for our participation in divine uncreated energies through Christ, not in the coming future but now. What does the Scripture say?

> For he spake in a certain *place* of the seventh day on this wise. And God did rest the seventh day from all his works. And in this *place* again, if they shall enter into my rest. . . . Again, he limiteth a certain day, saying in David, *Today*, after so long a time, as it is said, *Today*, if you will hear his voice, harden not your hearts. For if Jesus had given them rest, then would he not afterward have spoken of another day. There remaineth therefore a rest to the people of God. For he that is entered into his rest, he also hath ceased from his own works, as God did from his." (Heb 4:4–10)

The *place* is the KoGoE where divine (uncreated) energies become creative opportunities for God's equity and justice implementation through—and with—Christ who leads the co-creative endeavors.

CREATION OUT OF NOTHING:
KOGOE AS THE "NOTHING"

Both the Old Testament and New Testament teach that the universe was created out of nothing in the absolute sense. I see a possible relationship between KoGoE and "creation out of nothing." I suggest that KoGoE represents that "nothing" from which creation emerges. As such, KoGoE/nothing is not to be associated with the realms of the "infinite," or the "finite," nor is it something in-between. Hence, "Nothing/KoGoE" cannot belong to any category of

---

7. Palamas, as introduced in "Philokalia," [V4] 291.

empirical knowledge. The potential way to prove the existence of "nothing/KoGoe" is by the "just" consideration and measurement of its creative outcomes. This implies that God's act of creation out of absolute nothing/KoGoE may be proven through "Christ is fully with us."

GOD'S EQUITY AND JUSTICE: KOGOE IS FOR EVERYONE, KNOW THYSELF IS NOT MANDATORY

Inheriting from the wisdom traditions on purpose or not—like Ignatius and Luther themselves—the tools of the postmodern era make the complex quest for self-knowledge the starting point of human and social transformations. For example, in *Theory U*, self-knowledge is acquired through practices that include "listening, contemplation, mindfulness, social-emotional practices as well as presencing practices (to sense and actualize one's highest future potential)."[8] Similarly, contemporary tools such as Integral Spirituality heavily rely on self-knowledge and self-transcendence.[9] Given the target population that the latter serves—that is, aspiring self-actualizing individuals, such choice is not surprising. However, while the importance of self-knowledge is undeniable, I argue that it is not given to most of us to know—or just desire—to know ourselves, not to mention the impossibility of such a quest for those who have not been given that ability as a birthright. I further argue that an existential quest of that nature tends to accommodate a social category of people whom I qualify as "privileged" and to which I belong myself. With self-knowledge being an imperative prerequisite to human and social transformations, the "privileged" would always lead the movement which the "less privileged" are supposed to inherit or benefit from, one day. Such a situation is inconsistent with—nay contrary to—the principle of God's justice and equity, that depend on nothing but his/her unconditional love for everyone, not to human conditions, efforts, or merits.

8. Scharmer, "Vertical Literacy."
9. See Ken Wilber, "Actualize OS," https://actualizeos.com/.

The KoGoE is not only for the "privileged," i.e., the one who has learned how to listen, contemplate, think, feel and/or sense, or the self-actualizing individuals, albeit those traits are undeniably important. Rather, the KoGoE opens its door to everyone, including the non-Christian believers. Jesus states: "People will come from east and west and north and south, and will take their places at the feast in the kingdom of God" (Luke 13:29). On the same note, Paul claims: "Consequently, you [Gentiles] are no longer foreigners and strangers, but fellow citizens with God's people and also members of his household, built on the foundation of the apostles and prophets, with Christ Jesus himself as the chief cornerstone. In him, the whole building is joined together a rises to become a holy temple in the Lord. And in him, you too are being built together to become a dwelling in which God lives by his Spirit." (Eph 2:19–22). In brief, with/through/in "Christ is fully with us" everyone inherits the KoGoE. How can that be possible?

"CHRIST IS FULLY WITH US" AND ITS COMPONENTS

Drawing on Scripture and the sacred art of iconography, I suggest that "Christ is fully with us" serves as the foundation of the KoGoE where God's justice and equity reign on earth. "Christ is fully with us" reposes on four foundational elements: (1) the living Cross, (2) faith, (3) human stance, and (4) heartfulness.

The Living Cross

According to the Christian tradition, the cross symbolizes the Holy Trinity. As such, the cross is the vehicle of Trinitarian love for the human race through God's incarnation to human being, Christ's death, resurrection, and his sending of the Holy Spirit, i.e., the Spirit of Truth. Because of Christ's salvific act, anyone inherits the KoGoE by default (i.e., universal salvation).

Death

"Christ died for the salvation of us all. Now, the act of dying—giving oneself—for one's beloved is not exclusive to Christ. Although it rarely happened, we know of passionate lovers who literally died for the object of their love. Consequently, Christ's death cannot fully characterize the essence of His love for us. Rather, Christ's death made Him—only/just—fully human."[10] This introduces the necessity of his resurrection. To that we turn.

Resurrection

Resurrection symbolizes Christ's victory over death. In the KoGoE, those who believe and search for Christ in faith are provided with the gift of eternal life. Christ states: "I am the resurrection and the life. Whoever believes in me, though he dies, yet shall he live, and everyone who lives and believes in me shall never die" (John 11:25–26). Christ's resurrection connotes also life abundance. To the Samaritan who asks, "Are you greater than our father Jacob, which gave us the dwell, and drank from it himself, as did also his sons and his livestock?" Jesus answers, "Everyone who drinks this water will be thirsty again, but whoever drinks the water I give them will never thirst; Indeed the water I give them will become in them a spring of water welling up to eternal life" (John 4:13–14). He further adds, "I am the bread of life. Whoever comes to me will never go hungry, and whoever believes in me will never be thirsty" (John 6:35). In the KoGoE, we are invited to drink the water and eat the bread of everlasting life from and through the *living Cross*—that is, Christ. How do we respond?

---

10. Ralaiarisedy, "Re-opening the Gift of Justification-by-Faith," 82.

Faith as a Two-Step Iterative Process: "Intention" and "Action"

Faith expresses our *intention* to engage in personal relationship with Christ making use of at least one of the three foundational and ecumenical tools: (1) *reading of Scripture.* "The notion of scripture as a norm is a familiar one to Christian tradition, especially to Protestants";[11] (2) *meditative and contemplative prayers.* Concurring with the protestant tradition, Pope Francis added, "The best incentive for sharing the Gospel comes from contemplating it with love, lingering over its pages and reading it with the heart";[12] and (3) *the Sacrament of Eucharist.* In the Orthodox tradition, the church lives out the mystery of the Divine Economy in her sacramental life, with the Holy Eucharist at its center.[13]

Hence, through these three foundational and ecumenical tools, faith as *intention* keeps us open to the presence of "Christ is fully with us" while triggering the actualization of his gift of resurrection and eternal life in us. Faith becomes *action* when we receive that presence and use the *human stance* and *gifts*—that fit the moment or situation—to embody our personal relationship with Christ in order to positively affect the world around us in creative ways.

Human Stance

Human stance is our attitude toward life in the present moment. As such, human stance applies to those of us who have been given the ability to make decisions. We can choose between two stances, i.e., *Death* or *Life.* God revealed it to Moses in the Old Testament. "I have set before you life and death. . . . Now choose life, so that you and your children may live, and that you may love the Lord your God, listen to his voice, and hold fast to him. For the Lord is

---

11. Peters, God—the World's Future, 99.

12. Pope Francis, Evangelii Gaudium, 197.

13. Holy and Great Council, "Official Documents of the Holy and Great Council of the Orthodox Church."

your life" (Deut 30:19–20). Similarly, the prophet Jeremiah adds: "And to this people you shall say: 'Thus says the Lord: Behold, I set before you the way of life and the way of death'" (Jer 21:8).

In the New Testament, Christ shows a new "way": "I am the way, and the truth, and the life. No one comes to the Father except through me" (John 14:6). Now, we will see that Christ plays something of a balancing act whether we choose *Death* or *Life*.

- The human stance of *Death* pertains to everything that drains our energy such as guilt, lie, boredom, fear, etc. If we choose the stance of Death for some/any reason, we need to rely on faith. "Christ is fully with us" finds ways to unveil the truth about our life situation. He always knows what we need— even before we know it ourselves—and he cares. This is God's mystery of grace. Christ says: "I am the light of the world. Whoever follows me will have the light of life" (John 8:12).

- The human stance of *Life* pertains to human gifts that correspond to our realized and unrealized potentials. They are invigorating such as our passion, talent, skill, sensitivity, and/ or aspiration.

If we choose the stance of *Life*, Christ adds even more life energies to our life through our faith. This is another God's mysteries of grace. There is an exchange of creative energies between Christ and us, which we communicate and by which we benefit those around us, including those who cannot choose between death and life. We become co-creative partners while actualizing our human gifts (i.e., passion, skill, talent, sensitivity and aspiration) fully awakened through the resurrected Christ for the betterment of the world around us. For example, figure 8 is provided as an example of multiple iterations during the building of the hypothetical model of *Christ is fully with us in the KoGoE* (i.e., creative outcome). This example demonstrates the cooperation between "Christ is fully with us" and the human skills "abduction and deduction as modes of reasoning." According to Peirce (as cited in Yu), "Abduction is an exploratory data analysis that performs the function as a model builder. . . . It plays a role of explorer of viable

paths to further inquiry. . . . The goal is to explore the data, find a
pattern, and suggest a plausible hypothesis. . . . Deduction refines
the hypothesis based upon other plausible premises."[14] Peirce adds:
"Abduction is the only logical operation which introduces any new
idea."[15]

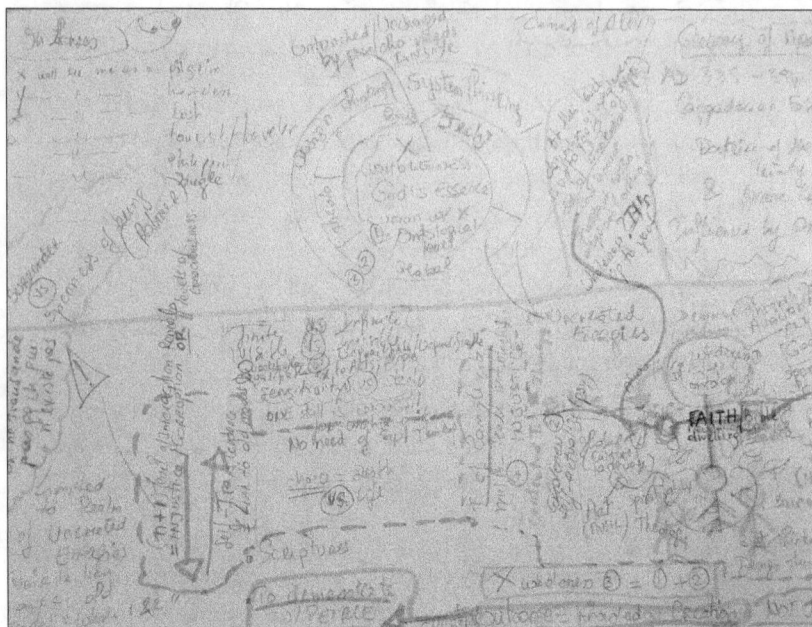

Figure 08. Example of human skills (i.e., modes of reasoning "abduction"
and "deduction") in cooperation with "Christ is fully with us."

On the other hand, according to Palamas, the divine energies
permeate the entire creation, and we humans participate in them
by grace. In other words, our human stance, the life-giving effect of
Christ as well as the creative energies that result from that life are
still dependent on God's grace. The potential conceptual overlap
that exists between Palamas's grace and Peirce's abductive mode of
reasoning merits a specific exploration which I will not undertake
in this book.

14. Yu, "Abduction? Deduction? Induction?"

15. Peirce, *Pragmatism and Pragmaticism*, 106.

Regardless of the above conversation, with "Christ is fully with us," we are *all* invited to live just as "how we are" in the Ko-GoE—not necessarily as "who we are" which is ontologically unknown for most of us—with the assurance of having Christ by our side, giving us hope and life energies. The symbolism of Orthodox iconography captures that Christian truth as follows: "The vibrant, flowering vines stretching out from the base of the Cross symbolize the life that comes to all men through the Wood of the Cross."[16]

Heartfulness: An "Intelligent Heart"

Theologians have attempted to shed light on the form of human's relation to God. For example, according to Siebenrock, a catholic theologian, Rahner attributes the latter to a "double movement:" (1) *kenosis*, i.e., the descent of God to the human (top down approach) and (2) *ecstasis*, i.e., the human's movement to God or transcendence (bottom up approach). In turn, the lutheran tradition proposes: "instead of our climbing the spiritual ladder to the top, God descends the ladder and meets us at the bottom."[17] On the contrary, I suggest that "Christ is fully with us" is neither a top-down nor a bottom-up, nor a combination of both, i.e., "double movement." Rather, "Christ is fully with us" is an expression of love toward the "other." Once we've learned to cultivate our relationship with God through Christ, we naturally attempt to engage in loving relationship with the world around us. Moreover, "Christ is fully with us" endows us with an "intelligent heart," i.e., a heart that both loves and knows the "truths" about the situation at hand. I call this inner movement of intelligent love toward the other *"heartfulness"* (i.e., "horizontal" multiplication). Through the third element of the Trinitarian love (i.e., Christ's sending of the Spirit of Truth), Christ leads us in that loving movement just as we are. In other words, he leads the path toward our individual appropriation of the KoGoE.

16. Fr. Bergenske, "Community of Joseph Icon Description."
17. Peters, *Sin Boldly: Justifying Faith for Fragile and Broken Souls*, 355.

THE SHIFT: CHOOSE LIFE,
SELF-KNOWLEDGE FOLLOWS

We are all invited in the KoGoE to be in relation with Christ—and co-create with/through him a just and beautiful world regardless of our self-knowledge, and/or level of belovedness, and/or our level of consciousness of God's love. John alluded to that Christian truth in his gospel: "And as Jesus passed by, he saw a man who was blind from his birth. And his disciples asked him, saying, Master, who did sin, this man or his parents, that he was born blind? Jesus answered, neither hath this man sinned, nor his parents: but that the work of God should be manifest in him" (John 9:1–3). In short, everyone has a role to play in the KoGoE. Christ is there, awaiting our response to his invitation to choose life no matter how much we know ourselves. *Self-knowledge unfolds as we choose life with/through Christ.* In other words, in the KoGoE, there is no requirement to go through the studious search for wholeness or belovedness in which self-knowledge is the point of entry to self-actualization. Instead, *"Christ is fully with us" leads to the actualization of our gifts* through/in/with Christ in the KoGoE. *As such, "Christ fully with us in the KoGoE" is the source of a paradigm shift in thinking about self and social transformations in the postmodern era.*

COULD "CHRIST IS FULLY WITH US"
BE THE JUSTIFYING FAITH?

As previously explained, "faith as the indwelling presence of Christ" is the faith that leads to our justification when it is combined with the hearing of the Word. In other words, from a theological standpoint, "faith as the indwelling presence of Christ" is intrinsically linked to justification as well as the hearing of the Word. On the contrary, "Christ is fully with us" is God's gift of relationship, offered to any of us—*de facto*—as a reflection of God's justice and equity in the KoGoE. It is at our disposal, here and now, before and after justification, through the Trinitarian love. This topic merits further exploration from a theological perspective, an endeavor that I will not undertake in this book.

BEYOND EXPECTED VALUE

In order to fully appreciate the effect of "Christ is fully with us" for the actualization of God's justice in the KoGoE, sound evaluation tools that include both the quantitative and qualitative aspects of the "creative outcome" need to be in place when the latter derives from the inheritance of eternal life through faith in Christ. New types of evaluation tool might be required for creative outcomes that derive from those who inherit both the eternal life and the Spirit of Truth. For that purpose, I would suggest the use of performative research. A practice-led research,

> "Performative Research" is an emerging approach to research in social science that is rooted in a social constructionist sensibility. . . . It emphasizes that the action of making and doing things by practicing artists, designers, inventors, architects and others who shape our sociomaterial world, should not just be seen as a subject for study using our traditional research methods, but should also be appreciated as unique research methods in their own right. . . . It reflects a pragmatist position that true knowledge is useful in action to achieve human goals and what constitutes a contribution to knowledge, is based on that usefulness, not its conformance to the web of preexisting theories and to elements of currently accepted ones. It says that if the outcome of our inquiries makes a difference in what we can achieve by new ways of acting, valuing or understanding the world, it is a valid research contribution.[18]

Lastly, we need to keep in mind that when Christ is fully with us, "creation out of the KoGoE" has surprises in store. Hence, the result exceeds human expectations.

---

18. Boland and Lyytinen, "Limits of Language in Systems Design," 248–49.

In the next chapter, I will provide an analysis of some of the barriers to our individual appropriation of "Christ is fully with us" in the context of higher education.

6

Challenges and Opportunities in the KoGoE

IN THE PREVIOUS CHAPTER, I suggested that with "Christ is fully with us," KoGoE is where "uncreated energies" become "creative opportunities" for making God's justice a reality here and now, not at the end of time. In other words, creative outcome is the first consequence of "Christ is fully with us" in the KoGoE. The nature of creative outcome depends on the human stance (i.e., life or death) and gifts (i.e., passion, talent, skill, sensitivity, aspiration). Using the context of the higher education where knowledge is the major outcome, I will explain some of the barriers to the individual appropriation of "Christ is fully with us" which, by the same occasion, impede the fulfillment of the KoGoE.

BROKENNESS OF THE CHURCH

"I give you a new commandment, that you love one another. Just as I have loved you, you also should love one another. By this, everyone would know that you are my disciples, if you have love for one another" (John 13:34–35). Jesus is clear about what he newly—or lastly—expects from his disciples. Right before the crucial moment of his crucifixion, he does not any longer reiterate the two Great Commandments. Rather, Jesus creates a new rule. He specifically commands his disciples to love one another as a proof of their Christian identity as well as their distinguishing mark of discipleship.

In the global and pluralistic world of the twenty-first century, Christianity faces the challenge of finding its identity and unifying characteristics. What does it mean to be a Christian in the postmodern world? Why are we Christians? To my knowledge, such a challenge primarily originates from a lack of true communion/unity among Christians. The Christian church of the postmodern world is both diverse and divided. While diversity enriches, division depletes. It is no secret; the church suffers from divisions of many natures. Chief among them is the division between the different Christian denominations: between Catholics, between Protestants, between Catholics and Protestants, between Christians of the West and those of the East. Using a metaphorical language, one can say, the members of the body of Christ are "broken down." Paul claims that members' unity is made possible only through Christ (1 Cor 12:12). Important works have been—and are being—undertaken not only for the unity of the church but also in relation to other religious traditions, as well as the natural sciences. Yet the new commandment calls for something different, or more. It calls for an authentic reconciliation within the separated Christian communities as a priority. This requires Christians' ability to engage in authentic "heart-to-heart" dialogue—i.e., dialogue from which incompatible and conflicting interests are removed—with their Christian brothers and sisters. In my opinion, those questions that are relevant to interreligious and interdisciplinary endeavors equally apply to the Christian communities. Jesus commands an approach that comes from "within." Indeed, how can Christians think of loving people from other traditions, of building peace, or caring for the environment if they do not get along with their closest sisters and brothers, namely, the Christians themselves? In other words, Jesus calls for the unity of the Christian communities as the first step toward the fulfillment of the Kingdom of God on Earth.[1]

UNHEALTHY COMPETITIVE BEHAVIORS

The brokenness of the church creates unhealthy competitions among the various church orders and theological schools. This leads to the loss of the ecclesial purpose. Indeed, the founders of the various Christian orders (e.g., Ignatius, Luther, Dominic, etc.) tend to become more important in the eyes of the church leaders and theologians than Christ himself.

LOSS OF THE FOUNDATIONAL ELEMENTS OF SOCIAL JUSTICE

In their book *Social Analysis: Linking Faith and Justice*, Henriot and Holland draw from the social teaching of the church to shed light on the power dynamics that influence organizational systems. To my knowledge, academic organizations are not prepared to respond to the three basic questions that the authors use for class and social analysis: (1) Who makes the decision (to produce "creative outcome" in the academic context here)? (2) Who benefits from the decision? (3) Who bears the cost of the decision?[2] Such analysis may shed light on the root causes of some of the challenges that relate to vocation. For example, why is it challenging to make a living with one's vocation when one is neither called to sisterhood or priesthood—nor to join a religious order? And to what extent do social and/or systemic injustices play a part in that situation? We often confuse God's trials with human injustice, putting all the blame on the former.

---

1. Ralaiarisedy, "Re-opening the Gift of Justification-by-Faith," 60–61.
2. Holland and Henriot, *Social Analysis*, 28.

OBSOLESCENCE OF THE ACADEMIC SYSTEMS

The academic systems present a number of characteristics that negatively impact our individual appropriation of "Christ is fully with us."

- Academic systems penalize creative thinking. Paradoxically, there is little room for experimentation of new thinking in the academic field. To my knowledge, one of the (well-known) reasons of such inadequacy pertains to the adoption of outdated research methods and academic rules that have become obsolete with the new types of research projects of multidisciplinary and cross-cultural natures that naturally emerged from the complexity of the postmodern world. An example of these creative "challengers" is the following kind of conversation: "You have new ideas? Great, but I recommend that you do what they ask you to do first." Such advice implies there might be a problem if your interest spans multiple disciplines. Then, the conversation continues: "Once you get your degree you can do what you want. . . ." Most creative people do not abide by those rules for they do not see "degree" as the primary motivation for engaging in academic endeavors. This is even truer for those who are in search for their vocation. I use a caricatural tone here and want to make sure that my remark is not understood as the rejection of the whole academic system. Not only do I not know the ins and outs of the academic system enough, but also I have enjoyed many aspects of the academic endeavor during my studies. The problem I point out is that after unsuccessful rebellious acts, some of the creative people give up and "conform" to the rules, or ran away to sustain their creative truth. I see this situation as a loss for both students and academic systems. In a chaotic postmodern world, we do not have any choice but to liberate the creative spirits.

- Academic systems lack transparency in relation to knowledge management. In their study of creative individuals, Stein and

Heinze reported one of the findings: "The author is concerned with certain injustices in British patent law which discourage the inventor and provide uncertain and inequitable financial rewards. . . . Although the law recognizes a special faculty that differentiates the inventor from 'persons skilled in the art,' he finds this faculty is not revealed by an examination of either the invention or the inventor."[3] While the finding pertains to the British system in the context of product invention, this issue is of a broad nature. To my knowledge, there is no specific process for the evaluation of creative outcomes. Consequently, the value that derives from creative outcomes cannot be measured in an *iterative* way and so is the consequence of "Christ is fully with us."

- Social technologies cannot be the answer. Social technologies do a good job at assessing the "creative outcome" which, in the context of the higher education, relates to knowledge and/ or advancement of knowledge in a given discipline. However, social technologies continue being silent, to my knowledge, on one point: they do not capture the "how the inventor's vision comes into being" before it translates into actionable insights, i.e., an example of creative outcome. Moreover, social technologies are built-up on self-knowledge. This is contrary to the whole principle of "Christ is fully with us" which transforms human gifts into creative opportunities rather than fostering self-actualization from self-knowledge, as described in the previous chapter.

DISREGARD FOR HUMAN DIGNITY

In *The Limits to Language in Doing Systems Design*,[4] Boland and Lyytinen use the lens of information systems to reveal the potential root causes of important academic discrepancies. While the article explores foundational issues in language and design in

---

3. Stein and Heinze, *Creativity and the Individual*, 245.

4. Boland and Lyytinen, "Limits to Language," 248–49.

information systems practice, it provides some clues on why such discrepancies may originate from the dismissing of human dignity and may lie beyond the mere obsolescence of academic systems.

The authors report West Churchman's—one of the interviewees—viewpoint as follows:

> What I must point out is how my discussions about reason, guarantors and the need for a sense of the whole system, have turned out to mask something even more important in my views on language and their limits—something that serves as my ontological grounding . . . —Reason, guarantors or a sense of whole are not the wellspring of my thinking—they are merely the best conclusion I can reach, using both logic and emotion. The wellspring for my thinking is the individual human being: the lonely, isolated, mortal, struggling, flesh and blood human being who makes choices and acts—that is what requires reason, a sense of whole and a guarantor. And that foundation of the singular, passionate, morally responsible and often anguished human being from which I draw my conclusions is missing from both [your] arguments. I am a humanist, pure and simple, and I am proud of it. I reject what both Latour and Bourdieu have said—realizing that they disagree between themselves quite strongly, but seeing each of them in their own way as having lost sight of the primacy of the individual. Latour . . . has made the individual disappear in favor of a circulating network of humans and artifacts, any node of which is subject to mediation and translations of interests. Bourdieu makes the individual disappear into recursively reproduced practices, where habits replace the passion and will of the singularly potent person. Give me the flesh and blood, the agonizing existential reality, of a human being facing the dread of everyday responsibilities. That's where I want to start. That is what is real: the individual human actor answering to God and the future of humankind for her actions.

Churchman's viewpoint reminds me of the universal value of human dignity. The Judeo-Christian tradition recognizes that the human person, as created in the image and likeness of God, is intrinsically a dignified creature. The disregard of the primacy of the individual equates to the disregard of human dignity and constitutes a barrier to the fulfillment of God's justice and equity in the KoGoE.

CARE FOR THE WHOLE PERSON:
A MISSED OPPORTUNITY

Ignatius of Loyola would agree with Churchman's statement. Ignatius made the "care for the whole person" (*cura personalis* in Latin) one of the foundational values of the Jesuit education.

> Originally used to describe the responsibility of the Jesuit Superior to care for each man in the community with his unique gifts, challenges, needs and responsibilities, this value [*Cura Personalis*] now is applied more broadly to include the relationship between educators and students and professionals relationships among all those who work in the academic environment, generally of Roman Catholic educational institutions.[5]

Cura Personalis is especially important in relation to the search for the "end for which we are created" for both priesthood and secular vocation. Hence, *cura personalis* ought to be openly promoted and fully extended to all students. Moreover, in the spirit of unity and ecumenism, *cura personalis* ought to be applied to theological schools of all denominations, not just the Catholic ones. It would differentiate seminaries and theological schools from other schools. A lack of appreciation for students' unique gifts, thus for human uniqueness is, in my opinion, one of the major impediments to the church edification in the postmodern world.

---

5. *Wikipedia.com*, s.v. "Cura personalis," https://en.wikipedia.org/wiki/Cura_personalis.

WRONG FOCUS ON THEOLOGICAL DEBATES

In the previous chapter, I drew attention to the primacy of God's gift of relationship with us through Christ. Since the fifth century, the doctrine of Chalcedon that states, "Christ is fully divine and fully human," has been the subject of debates and divergences among theologians. While this doctrine is of most importance from theological perspectives, it *cannot*—and is not meant to—address, in my opinion, the immediate need of Christian believers in the postmodern era. Consequently, it does not help towards the fulfillment of the KoGoE. Indeed, with the richness brought by multiculturalism, globalization, interreligious dialogue, and technologies, Christian believers increasingly express the desire to know what does it mean to be Christians and why is it important? Moreover, the focus on the Chalcedonian doctrine may reveal an actual lack of knowledge of what it actually means to have Christ's full presence with us. In other words, it may imply that we can only theologize about Christian truths when we actually experience them.

CULTURE CANNOT INFLUENCE OUR INDIVIDUAL APPROPRIATION OF "CHRIST IS FULLY WITH US"

There is a tendency to promote multiculturalism in the church at large today. This translates into the multiplication of opportunities for education and immersion into other cultures, religions and spiritual traditions. Whereas such initiatives were previously under the wings of interreligious and culturally specialized organizations, they have become part of ecclesial activities and offerings. Without any doubt, cultural literacy fosters human ability for tolerance and peace, to name but a few of their benefits. Yet, I find it important to point out that culture cannot influence our individual appropriation of "Christ is fully with us." Only faith does. Culture can only influence our understanding and expression of this God's grace and Christian mystery. This emphasizes the primacy of the cultivation of our personal relationship with Christ—as an act of faith—over cultural literacy, in the context of ecclesial education. As I stated in the previous chapter, *faith* expresses our *intention* to engage in personal relationship with Christ through one or all of the foundational and ecumenical tools—i.e., reading of Scripture, meditative prayers, and the sacrament of Eucharist—in order to actualize his gift of resurrection and eternal life in us. Hence, *faith* keeps us open to the presence of "Christ is fully with us." Faith becomes *action* when we receive that presence and use the *human stance* and *gifts*—that fit the moment or the situation—to embody our personal relationship with Christ. This iterative process of "faith as intention-action" affects the world around us in positive ways, leading to the actualization of God's justice and equity in the KoGoE.

7

Gratitude

THIS BOOK IS THE result of human and divine interconnectedness with its risks, challenges, and beauties.

Over the past decade, the following people crossed my path and touched my heart with their kindness: Connie Anderson, Maya Apolinario, Vassilis Backos, Pavel Baklanov, Ed and Esther Bourg, Didier Cabannes, Adrienne Delbecq-Backos, Vicky Chamilou, Solange Charras, Daryl Conner, Carla de Sola, Theodosis Diakogiannis, Amy Erickson, Ersilia Foglia, Shanit Gupta, Sandra Hietala, Monica Hove, Lise-Lotte Iversen, Arvind Jodi, Stéphanie Jufas, Janie Kail, Katerina Kakiori, Efterpi Karounou, Byron Kennedy, Yiannis Mathiasos, Zdravka Mihaylova, Charles Milo, Maryann Montandon, Rebecca Morris, Scarlet Nickhol, Peter M. Phleger, Eric Quan, Christian Rakotondratsima, Brian Robertson, Pravina Rodriguès, Sandra Russum, Julie Sadowski, Vassia Sarri, Suzy Switzer, Kirsten Tasker, Jola Isufi Vasili, Kim Wayne, Terry Watters, Gail Whipple, and Stavros Yangazoglou. I am deeply thankful to each and every one of you.

I am grateful to my academic advisors and teachers for the crucial roles they played on my path: Laurie MacPherson and Kathleen Kane (University of San Francisco) introduced me to the relationship between spirituality, leadership and creativity; Richard Boland (Case Western Reserve University) instilled my interest in research methods; Dana Greene (Evelyn Underhill Association) reinforced my understanding of the purpose of God's love through the work of Evelyn Underhill on mysticism; Cindy Wigglesworth (Deep Change, Inc.) broadened my understanding of spirituality through her teaching on Spiritual Intelligence; Rick Jarrow enriched my understanding of vocation through his lecture on "Your life's work: the ultimate anti-career guide;" Frère Romain (Ecole Sacré-Coeur d'Antanimena) accompanied me with his Orémus; Sister Sue Mosteller (Sisters of St. Joseph of Toronto) deepened my understanding of Henri Nouwen's teaching on God's love; Sister Barbara Green (Dominican School of Philosophy and Theology, Graduate Theological Union) opened for me a vital creative space during my first year of biblical studies. Ted Peters (Pacific Lutheran Theological Seminary, Center for Theology and the Natural Sciences, Graduate Theological Union) provided me with a rich exposure to the Lutheran scholarship as well as the relationship between science and religion. Alison Benders (Jesuit School of Theology, Graduate Theological Union) showed me the way of academic persistence and patience; Seth Godin encouraged me to "leap first" with care.

I am grateful to the communities that nurtured my faith in many beautiful ways over the past decade: New Vision United Methodist Church of Millbrae, Jesuit Retreat Center of Los Altos, United Religions Initiative, Brahma Kumaris of San Francisco, First Presbyterian Church of Burlingame, Mercy Center Burlingame, Eglise Saint-Sulpice (Paris), Community of Joseph (Santa Clara University), United Church of Christ of San Mateo, Chapel of the Jesuit School of Theology of Berkeley, First Christian Church of San Jose, House Church (Berkeley), First Presbyterian Church of Berkeley, Holy Spirit Newman Hall of Berkeley, Christ Church of Berkeley, University Lutheran Chapel of Berkeley, Peninsula Bible Church (Palo Alto), Eglise Protestante Unie de France en Vallée de l'Orge, Notre-Dame de Dusenbach (Ribeauvillé), Temple Luthérien (Ribeauvillé), Orthodox Church of the Nativity of the Blessed

Virgin Mary (Kardamena), St. Paul's Anglican Church of Athens, Holy Monastery of Saint-John the Baptist (Kareas), Church of Agios Nikolaos (Kaisariani), and the editors of "Parole pour Tous" (Editions SMPP). The gift of these communities has been—and will always be—a vital part of my journey. I am especially grateful to Giannis Papavieros for his selfless and joyful service to the church.

I am indebted to Fr. Jim Manney, Fr. Joe Fice, the late Professor André Delbecq, Fr. Gregory Mayers, Sr. Jane Ferdon, Fr. George Murphy, and Mary Manning for their priceless gift of spiritual guidance.

I am thankful to Wipf and Stock Publishers for their patient waiting while I was "getting ready" for the completion of this manuscript. Their presence has been instrumental in sustaining my whole journey. I especially thank Christian Amondson, Matthew Wimer, Daniel Lanning, Zechariah Mickel, Karl Coppock, and George Callihan for assisting me throughout the publication process. I am further thankful to Mary and Jim Manning for their constructive criticism and proofreading of the manuscript.

I am grateful to Francis Rousseaux and Amel Caltagirone for "introducing" me to Greece, i.e., the country in which this book came into fruition. Louise Todd Cope, Anne-Marie Duliège, Valérie Duvillier, David Keim, Sally Mahé, Jim Manning, Mary Manning, and Elisa de Martel have been core supporters in joy and sorrow. I am grateful for their sustaining friendship. I am further appreciative to Louise for keeping the light on through her creative work.

And finally, I would not have completed the writing of this book in the best possible conditions without the loving presence of my family. My deep gratitude goes to my son Michael who offered his unconditional support in many ways. The whole family (i.e., my parents, my sisters and brothers, my aunts and uncle, my nieces, nephews, and cousins) helped sustain my faith with their love, laughters, and prayers. You are the salt and light of my daily life. Thank you dear Ones!

Bibliography

Bergenske, Theodore. "Community of Joseph Icon Description." Excerpt from informal, standalone document created for the Community of Joseph on behalf of its founder, André Delbecq. 2002.

Boland, Richard, Jr., and Lyytinen, Kalle. "The Limits to Language in Doing Systems Design." *European Journal of Information Systems* 26 (2017) n.p. https://doi.org/10.1057/s41303-017-0043-4.

Boyatzis, R. E., et al. "The Ideal Self as the Driver of Intentional Change." *Journal of Management Development* 25 (2006) 624–42.

Fassett, Edward S., et al. "Moved to Greater Love." https://jesuits.org/greaterlove.

Fleming, David. *Draw Me into Your Friendship: The Spiritual Exercises.* Literal translation and contemporary reading. St Louis: Institute of Jesuit Sources, 1996.

George, Bill, et al. *True North: Discover Your Authentic Leadership.* San Francisco: Wiley, 2007.

Holland, J., and P. Henriot. *Social Analysis: Linking Faith and Justice.* Rev. ed. New York: Orbis, 1983.

Holy and Great Council. Official Documents of the Holy and Great Council of the Orthodox Church. Message of the Holy and Great Council of the Orthodox Church. Pentecost 2016. https://www.holycouncil.org/-/message.

Luther, Martin. *Luther's Works.* Vol. 25, *Lectures on Romans.* Edited by Hilton C. Oswald. St. Louis: Concordia House, 1972.

———. *Luther's Works.* Vol. 26, *Lectures on Galatians 1535.* Chapters 1–4. Edited by Jaroslav Pelikan and Walter A. Hansen. St. Louis: Concordia House, 1963.

Palamas, Gregory. "Introductory Note." In *Philokalia*, introduced and translated by G. E. H. Palmer et al. 1977. https://www.holybooks.com/wp-content/uploads/Philokalia.pdf.

Palmer, Parker. *Let Your Life Speak: Listening for the Voice of Vocation.* San Francisco: Jossey-Bass, 1999.

Peirce, C. Sanders. *Pragmatism and Pragmaticism.* Edited by Charles Harstshorne and Paul Weiss. Collected Papers 5. Cambridge: Belknap, of Harvard University Press, 1960.

Peters, Ted. *God—the World's Future: Systematic Theology for a New Era.* 3rd ed. Minneapolis: Fortress, 2015.

―――. *Sin Boldly: Justifying Faith for Fragile and Broken Souls.* Minneapolis: Fortress, 2015.

Pigeaud, Olivier, and Danielle Vergniol. "Parole pour Tous." Editions SMPP. www.editions-smpp.com.

Pope Francis. *Evangelii Gaudium.* Apostolic exhortation on the proclamation of the gospel in today's world. Vatican, 2013. http://m.vatican.va/content/francescomobile/en/apost_exhortations/documents/papa-francesco_esortazione-ap_20131124_evangelii-gaudium.html.

Rahner, Karl. *Discours d'Ignace de Loyola aux Jesuites d'Aujourd'hui.* Translated by Charles Elhinger. Paris: Centurion, 1979.

Ralaiarisedy, Hanitra. "Re-opening the Gift of Justification-by-Faith: A Fresh Look at Reformation." MA thesis (undefended), Graduate Theological Union, 2018.

Saint-Exupéry, Antoine de. *Wind, Sand and Stars.* Translated by Lewis Galantière. New York: Harcourt, Brace, 2002.

Saint Ignatius Loyola. *A Pilgrim's Journey: The Autobiography of St. Ignatius of Loyola.* Introduction, translation, commentary by Joseph N. Tylenda. San Francisco: Ignatius, 2001.

Scharmer, Otto. "Vertical Literacy: Reimagining the 21st Century University." *Medium,* April 15, 2019. https://medium.com/presencing-institute-blog/vertical-literacy-12-principles-for-reinventing-the-21st-university-39c2948192ee.

Schillebeeckx, Edward. *Revelation and Theology.* London: Sheed and Ward, 1967.

Stein, Morris, and Shirley Heinze. *Creativity and the Individual.* Glencoe, IL: Free Press, 1960.

Thibodeaux, Mark. *God's Voice Within: The Ignatian Way to Discover God's Will.* Chicago: Loyola Press, 2010.

Walgrave, H. Jan. *Unfolding Revelation: The Nature of Doctrinal Development.* Philadelphia: Westminster, 1972.

Yu, Ho. "Abduction? Deduction? Induction? Is There a Logic of Exploratory Data Analysis?" https://www.coursehero.com/file/26767169/EDA-inferencedoc.